WOMEN POLICE OFFICERS

CURRENT CAREER PROFILE

ABOUT THE AUTHOR

Patricia Lunneborg received her Ph.D. in psychology from the University of Texas in Austin in 1962. She taught from 1967 to 1988 at the University of Washington during which time she published over 100 professional publications, principally concerning women's career development.

WOMEN POLICE OFFICERS

CURRENT CAREER PROFILE

By

PATRICIA W. LUNNEBORG, Ph.D.

Retired Professor
Psychology and Women's Studies
University of Washington
Seattle, Washington

CHARLES C THOMAS • PUBLISHER
Springfield • Illinois • U.S.A.

Published and Distributed Throughout the World by

CHARLES C THOMAS • PUBLISHER
2600 South First Street
Springfield, Illinois 62794-9265

© *1989 by* CHARLES C THOMAS • PUBLISHER

ISBN 0-398-05623-4

Library of Congress Catalog Card Number: 89-5187

With THOMAS BOOKS *careful attention is given to all details of manufacturing
and design. It is the Publisher's desire to present books that are satisfactory as to their
physical qualities and artistic possibilities and appropriate for their particular use.*
THOMAS BOOKS *will be true to those laws of quality that assure a good name
and good will.*

Printed in the United States of America
SC-R-3

Library of Congress Cataloging-in-Publication Data

Lunneborg, Patricia W.
  Women police officers : current career profile / by Patricia W.
Lunneborg.
    p. cm.
  Includes bibliographical references.
  ISBN 0-398-05623-4
  1. Policewomen—United States. I. Title.
HV8143.L85 1989
363.2'023'73—dc20   89-5187
                                                                            CIP

PREFACE

Women have slowly but steadily increased their representation in police ranks in the 1970s and 1980s. In 1980 women were 5 percent of all sworn officers in the U. S., and by 1987, 7.6 percent, according to the FBI's *Uniform Crime Reports*.

This steady, if slow, progress means there is increasing interest in women becoming police officers. It also suggested to me that there probably now existed enough research studies on women police for a book. That was my original intent: to summarize the scholarly research literature on women police written in the 1980s.

The fact is that there were not enough scholarly, empirical research investigations to fill these pages. Hence, I revised my plan and reviewed the professional and popular literature on women police as well. I have also added a few good foreign studies and studies about criminal justice students, officers-to-be. And even though a particular study was published in the 1980s doesn't mean the data were collected then. Several studies look like they are recent, when in fact the data are from the 1970s.

In the end, my intention became to integrate all these disparate publications in order to present the fullest possible portrait of the U. S. woman police officer today. And while originally my only purpose was to inform and describe, I adopted a second purpose as I wrote: to encourage more research on women police. This book is hardly definitive. It is, instead, what the evidence suggests women police are like.

The *purpose* of this book, then, is to meet the needs of several audiences for information on the career of the woman police officer. What are those audiences?

Perhaps the most important is, simply, women-in-general who are working or planning work in poorly paid, traditional women's occupations. They need down-to-earth facts about the police service as a career.

There is no doubt that policing is an area of opportunity for women today. For minority women as well as white women. For high school graduates as well as college graduates. For women in their thirties as well as in their twenties. In addition to better wages and benefits compared to teaching, nursing, secretarial and clerical work, not to speak of unskilled service and factory jobs, a career with the police offers interesting assignments, job security and decent pay, and a continual challenge to meet the serious social needs of urban American society.

This book is also for the 40,000 and rising women patrol officers and detectives who deserve a timely summary of their progress and achievements. They merit an integration of the sociological and psychological studies in which they participated. They've earned the right to a collective portrait, to know as much about themselves as police scientists and law enforcement experts, not to speak of sympathetic journalists, have learned.

Another women's audience consists of women's studies scholars. Many are wary of the police and military, but they know only too well that deep cultural change in the established mores, values, and traditions of these two occupations will only come about when these fields are no longer male-dominated. What are the values and approaches of women attracted to the police? What can we look forward to as women become a greater presence in the police service?

Two other audiences for this book consist for the most part of men. There are government administrators, especially police chiefs, who know that one answer to their police personnel problems is successful recruitment and retention of women. Affirmative action and equal employment opportunity are philosophies not only to benefit women, but to benefit employers, by tapping the most underutilized and promising resource in criminal justice today.

There are also law enforcement instructors. Police science is a growing field and more and more colleges are offering undergraduate and graduate degrees in criminal justice and law enforcement. Instructors at these colleges, as well as at police academies, can use this book as a source as well as to encourage more and better research on women in policing.

The *scope* of this book is broad. It gathers together a considerable body of knowledge published in the 1980s on women police which is spread over many, diverse sources. Empirical research investigations, expert observations, case studies alike are reviewed. They come from scholarly journals, professional magazines, and popular literature as well. Sometimes there is more wisdom, knowledge, and truth in the lifetime observations of a single individual, or in the in-depth interviews of 25 people, than there is in 800 empirical one-page surveys.

The **Plan:** An opening chapter sketches a brief history of women officers in American law enforcement, including a review of the civil rights legislation of the 1970s which enabled greater numbers of women to enter police work. Next, a perspectives chapter summarizes and critiques the evaluative research of the 1970s which focused primarily on the question of whether women were competent to perform general patrol duties. Following this are ten chapters devoted to what the woman officer is like, in her background, family, lifestyles. Her personality, values, attitudes, and occupational interests. What are her job motivations, her job satisfactions? What are her particular job stresses and ways of coping? Her style of policing? Perceptions of her performance compared to others' perceptions? What is important to retaining women, and how have they fared in supervision and promotion? What impact have they made on policing? And last, what research directions should we take in the 1990s?

The literature of the 1980s, on the surface, seems to focus on what everyone thinks about the performance of women police. Some 1980s' themes are the resistant attitudes of the police organization itself, men's negative opinions about women police, and the continuing slow progress made in getting women into the service. But beneath the male resistance and sex discrimination are facts about *what women police are like, how they live, how they think,* and this can be presented from a positive, balanced perspective. This is what I aim to do.

If more women are directly encouraged to explore police work, and more men encouraged to support them in that exploration, the book will accomplish one of its missions. And when this "current career profile" is updated, if I find hundreds of new studies to read and think about, it will have accomplished its second mission.

I would like to express my appreciation to the following for their substantial contributions to the book: Professor Donald Zytowski of Iowa State University, Sgt. Barbara Hauptman of Omaha, Nebraska, and Cathie Jones of San Diego. Additionally, I greatly appreciated the support of Major Beryl Thompson, recently retired from the Seattle Police Department, Captain Michael Germann at Seattle's Criminal Justice Training Center, Chief Michael Shanahan, University of Washington Police Department, and my favorite graduate school instructor, Professor Emeritus Ezra Stotland, former Director of the University of Washington's Society and Justice Program.

CONTENTS

WOMEN POLICE OFFICERS

CURRENT CAREER PROFILE

Chapter 1

INTRODUCTION

"How Good Are Women Cops?" How many times have we read that headline in a newspaper or magazine? It was how Tom Seligman introduced his article on women police in a March 31, 1985 issue of *Parade Magazine* that came with our *Seattle Times.*

Seligman's major message was that women had humanized police departments across the country and shown how it was possible to be gentle and compassionate and still be a good cop. He touched on several topics to prove his point and these are still the questions most asked by people interested in women who become police officers. He asked . . .

Why do women want to become police officers?

What work experience do women typically have when they come to policing?

How do law enforcement executives evaluate women police?

How does the public react to women police?

How do male colleagues feel about women police?

What is the impact of the job on the women's personal lives and families?

What are the job satisfactions of a police career for women?

How do women change who become police officers?

Do women have a different style of law enforcement?

What are some of the impacts women have made on police departments?

This book presents some tentative answers to these ten questions. It represents a collective portrait of American women police officers, based on contemporary professional, popular, and scholarly literature of the 1980s. Before we get to this literature, however, first a bit of history.

THE 1920S TO THE 1960S: WOMEN ENTER THE POLICE

When did women first become police officers in the United States? Why were they hired? What did they do? What were they like?

There were women on board the police service as early as 1845 in New

3

York City, if the job of jail matron qualifies as police officer. If matrons aren't *real* police, then the first woman called a "police officer" (actually "patrolman") but without arrest powers was Marie Owens, appointed by the mayor of Chicago in 1893. Mrs. Owens, the widow of a patrolman, chiefly assisted male detectives in cases involving women and children.

If arrest powers are the critical factor, even if they go with the title "safety worker," then Lola Baldwin may be the first woman police officer. She was hired by Portland, Oregon in 1905 to look after women and children at the Lewis and Clark Exposition. In that same year Portland became the first city in the U. S. to organize a Women's Division in its police department. But if *both* title and being a sworn officer with the power to arrest are needed to be the first woman police officer, then it is Alice Stebbins Wells hired by Los Angeles in 1910.

Although Alice Wells was hired as a police officer, she spent a lot of her time away from L. A. drumming up support for the hiring of women officers throughout the rest of the country. She spoke in as many as 31 cities in 30 days, so that by 1915 policewomen were working in twenty-five cities in twenty states. That same year saw the founding of the International Association of Police Women (IAPW), now known as the International Association of Women Police (IAWP). And, in the year before, Dolly Spencer was appointed by the mayor of Milford, Ohio, as America's first woman Chief of Police. Mrs. Spencer got rid of the town's gambling problem by raiding the gamblers' dens, and taking the young offenders to her home where she turned them over to their parents.

By the end of World War I there were women police in more than 200 U. S. cities. Their acceptance was solidified in 1922 when the International Association of Chiefs of Police proclaimed that women were essential members of the modern police department.

Throughout this early period the role of women in policing was strictly a specialist one. Why that was true is linked with how women gained entry into police work in the first place — the early women's movement. Alice Wells' proselytizing had the support of countless private women's groups, for example, the American Female Reform Society, the Women's Christian Temperance Union, the League of Women Voters. It was pressure from women upon city and state governments to hire first, police matrons, and then, police officers, that allowed women to prove their worth.

The rationale for hiring women, a rationale advanced foremost by women themselves, was that there were certain aspects of police work which are inappropriate for men to perform. The rationale maintained that women were especially suited to specific tasks and had a special contribution to make. Women were argued to be uniquely qualified to deal with cases involving women and children; they were likewise skilled at defusing family fights and doing undercover work on vice squads that called for women. And men were happy to argue that women, "naturally," were better at routine clerical details.

These first women police, matrons and sworn officers alike, tended to be upper-middle class, well-educated, reform-minded social workers. They were service-oriented, they were idealists. They had no trouble arguing that they were better than men at social welfare tasks because of women's presumed natural tendencies and abilities. While they needed to do patrol work in order to fulfill their social work mission, they preferred to do so in plainclothes. They visited dance halls, skating rinks, and theaters, and dealt with prostitutes and runaways. They operated their patrols through separate women's bureaus and, in some instances, out of different locations, such as the famous 1920s "Women's Precinct" in New York City's Hell's Kitchen. The women police of this era did not feel they were "real cops," they were social workers. But, to them, "true" police work was social work.

Mary Hamilton (1924), hired as New York City's first regular woman police officer, wrote in *The Policewoman: Her Service and Ideals,* that the position of woman in a police department is like that of a mother in a home (p. 4). Women are necessary to the police, she felt, because prevention and protection are essential parts of police work. And what women learn from being mothers, they can use to look out for the welfare of others. Thus, women police should prevent women and girls from becoming criminals, not only for their own sakes, but because it protects the next generation from crime as well.

Mrs. Hamilton believed that the profession of policewoman would become as standardized, universal, and necessary as the nursing profession in fifty years time. She also predicted the "correct" number of women in the service would be one percent (p. 34), a puzzling standard, given the percentage of women in the general population, and the number of women who are victims of crime, even if one believes that women's moral superiority protects them from becoming criminals.

We certainly can't blame Mrs. Hamilton for what happened over the next forty years, but that one percent became the norm. Up to the mid-1960s U. S. police departments maintained this small quota of women to handle women and children and clerical duties. Why?

Peter Horne (1980, pp. 31–32) believes economics were responsible. He points to the collapse of the policewomen's movement at the same time as the stock market crash of 1929 and to the decimation of women's ranks during the Great Depression. Hiring stayed at a standstill until World War II. Then, after women had filled in for men during the war, again they were let go. As a result, Horne says, the situation was the same for women through the 1950s and 1960s as it had been in the 1920s. Women continued to occupy a specialized, extremely marginal place in American policing. It was not until the late 1960s that the movement revived.

THE 1960S AND 1970S: SOME SPECIAL WOMEN

Two very special women were Felicia Shpritzer and Gertrude Schimmel. Two Hunter College graduates destined *not* to become school teachers. Two important women in the history of the police. Alice Fleming (1975, p. 221) calls Shpritzer "Lieutenant Nerve," and Schimmel "Inspector Brains." Because together they were the brains and the nerve that won the fight for promotion of women in the New York City Police Department.

In 1961 Shpritzer, a policewoman since 1942, sued the chairman of New York City's Civil Service Commission because it had turned down her application to take the exam for sergeant. She and Gertrude Schimmel, who had entered the force in 1940, served and waited and served and waited in the Juvenile Aid Division for more than twenty years for their first promotion. The legal process itself took 2 years, 3 court cases, and 13 judges before the police and the city of New York were convinced that women deserved an equal right to fail the sergeant's exam. In 1964 Shpritzer and Schimmel took that exam and passed.

Gertrude Schimmel was the first woman to take and pass all three civil service exams — sergeant, lieutenant, and captain — and to become, in 1971, the first woman deputy inspector in the New York City Police Department.

In Horne's opinion (1980, p. 34), the determination of two other, special women, "perhaps more than anything else," marked the end of the old order. The two, Betty Blankenship and Elizabeth Coffal, finally talked the chief of the Indianapolis Police Department into letting them do general patrol duty in a radio car, Car 47, in September 1968. They were grudgingly accepted by the men when they proved they could handle the job. It was a real breakthrough.

The most special woman of the 1970s was a 24-year-old black mother of a young child, Officer Gail A. Cobb of the Metropolitan Police Department of Washington, DC. She was shot to death by a bank robbery suspect on September 20, 1974. She was the first woman police officer killed in the line of duty in the U. S. It's said that Officer Cobb's death ironically helped the cause of women police because it proved to men police that women were prepared to die and were dying along side of them. In 1988 of the 153 officers killed on duty, eight were women.

To conclude, both during the 1920s, when women entered policing, and during the 1960s and early 1970s when women entered patrol work, two forces were responsible. An active women's movement on the one hand and assertive, ambitious, individual women on the other. However, another force joined these two in the 1970s which aided the acceptance of women into general police work and brought into question their being relegated to specialist roles.

THE 1970S: THE IMPACT OF CIVIL RIGHTS LEGISLATION

The year 1972, was according to Horne (1980, pp. 32–35), the start of The Modern Era for women police. Lots of things happened that year. ERA was proposed by a two-thirds vote of Congress, the FBI appointed its first female Special Agent, and women went out on patrol in Washington, DC and New York City for the first time.

Perhaps the most important thing that happened was that Congress passed the Equal Opportunity Act of 1972. This expanded the coverage of Title VII of the Civil Rights Act of 1964 to include *public* as well as private employers. State and local government agencies, including police departments, were prohibited from employment practices which discriminated on the basis of race, creed, color, national origin, *or sex.*

Under the provisions of Title VII the Equal Employment Opportunity Commission (EEOC) was created in 1968 as the federal regulatory agency responsible for monitoring compliance with the law. It was the EEOC's function to see that any job was open to both men and women unless it could be proven that sex was a bona fide occupational qualification (BFOQ). Now to justify discriminatory requirements, employers had to show that discrimination was necessary for the safe and efficient operation of a business.

An additional piece of civil rights legislation that benefitted women police even more directly was the Crime Control Act of 1973. This Act amended the Omnibus Crime Control and Safe Streets Act of 1968 so that any police agency discriminating against women could not receive grant money from the Law Enforcement Assistance Administration (LEAA). And LEAA's money was considerable. One billion dollars a year went to improve 40,000 departments, courts, and correctional facilities. Unfortunately, LEAA, born in 1968, died in 1983, and with it this additional pressure to implement women's equal opportunity plans.

THE 1980S:
CURRENT STATUS OF WOMEN POLICE OFFICERS

Numbers

Depending on which part of government the statistics come from, the numbers of women police are different. What the statistics all agree on, however, is that the proportion of women keeps increasing.

The FBI's *Uniform Crime Reports,* produced annually by the Department of Justice, shows a gradual rise among all agencies from 5 percent in 1980, close to 20,000 women, to 7.6 percent in 1987, representing over 36,000 women. On the other hand, the "police and detectives, public service" counted by the Current Population Survey of the Bureau of Labor Statistics were 9.2 percent women in 1987, or 40,000 women.

The Bureau of Labor Statistics (1988b) has projected that overall the number of sworn officers, women and men, will increase by about 17 percent between 1986 and 2000. Thus, the total number of women in the police might be above 50,000 by the end of the century.

There are also expert projections about the number of women police in the future. For example, one expert predicted that by the year 2000 women would be 30 percent of all police agency personnel, and 10 percent of all command staffs (Ammann, 1981). My own guess would be that the increase of women will continue to be one-half to one percent per year, so that the number of female sworn officers by 2000 might just reach 20 percent.

Regional Differences

Are there regional differences in the proportion of women in the police service? Are some states and cities better than others in their commitment to affirmative action and increasing women's opportunities to police? Yes.

A 1981 national survey of police chiefs in 254 cities of 25,000 or more people revealed that the West and South are much better about hiring women than the Northcentral or Northeast regions (Steel and Lovrich, 1987).

First, the chiefs indicated the degree of priority they assigned to recruiting women into the police. The percentages who said women's recruitment was "top priority" or "important but not top priority" were the West 78 percent, South 64 percent, Northeast 58 percent, and Northcentral, 57 percent.

Then the chiefs supplied actual data to support their verbal commitment. The authors looked at the four regions in 1978 and 1981 in terms of the number of women sworn officers as a percentage of the officer workforce. Departments were categorized as having 0 to 2%, 3–5%, 6–8%, or 9 or more percent women.

Here are the percentages of departments having 6 percent or more women in 1981: South 44%, Northcentral 29%, West 23%, and Northeast 17%. (These regions have exactly the same order—South highest with Northeast lowest—in terms of the percentages of *black* women officers in 1979 as reported by Townsey, 1982a.)

The above figures should also be compared to the following percentages of departments which had the smallest proportions (0–2%) of women in 1981: South 18%, West 24%, Northcentral 35%, and Northeast 64%.

A third important aspect to these data is the degree of progress made between 1978 and 1981. The South made the most progress, followed by the West, the Northcentral region, and last, the Northeast.

Steel and Lovrich speculate that the good track record in the West correlates with the tradition of women's rights in these states which were the first to give women the vote and institute community property rights in marriage. They were surprised at the high rate of women's employment and rate of increase in the utilization of women in the South, and gave the expanding economic picture of the "sunbelt states" as the reason. The same economic argument in reverse was said to account for the low usage of women in Northeastern and Northcentral cities, although the authors thought that strong police unions in these regions also might have something to do with it.

State Differences

The FBI's *Uniform Crime Reports* also tell us how many sworn state police and highway patrol officers are women. The states vary greatly. In 1987, for example, Idaho had 140 men working for the state police and one woman. Wyoming also had one woman out of 149 officers. California had the most women, 353 to 5,137 men (6 percent women). New York State employed 3,729 men and 179 women (5 percent). But while New York and California employed the most women in absolute numbers, other states did better in terms of proportions, for example, the Florida Highway Patrol with 7 percent women and the Wisconsin State Patrol with 11 percent women.

City Differences

I've already indicated that in 1987 the proportion of women sworn officers nationwide was 7.6 percent. But the *Uniform Crime Reports* also look at the rates for different sized cities, and big cities have higher rates of employment of women police than small cities. In 1987 the eight U. S. cities with a million or more inhabitants had 11 percent women, the 60 cities with a quarter million or more inhabitants, 10.4 percent women. In contrast, the 6,518 cities with under 10,000 inhabitants had only 5 percent women officers.

Even among cities of the same size, there is considerable variability. Hochstedler, Regoli, and Poole (1984) present data on women for nineteen major city police agencies for 1981. The mean percentage of women across all nineteen cities was 6 percent. But they ranged from highs of 10 percent in Atlanta and Kansas City to lows of 3 percent in New Haven, New York, and St. Louis. The top five cities in 1981, in terms of achieving affirmative action for women, according to these researchers' figures, were Atlanta, Kansas City, Washington, DC, Detroit, and San Francisco.

The differences among cities in Hochstedler et al.'s findings also pointed to the South and West being better at hiring women and the Northeast being less receptive.

Rank

How many women police officers are above the rank of patrol officer? Potts (1981) says that only 5.3 percent of sworn women in thirty-nine large departments in 1978 were in supervisory or command grades. He also illustrates the enormous variation that exists among departments with a table showing that 12 of the 39 cities had no women at all in command grades. Some of the better cities were Fort Worth with 11 percent women, Newark with 14 percent, and Seattle with 15 percent. They were "better" not only because of having a higher percentage of women than 5.3, but because the discrepancy between the percentage of women in command positions was not grossly out of line with the percentage of *all* officers in command. For example, Memphis had 13 percent women in command, however overall 40 percent of its sworn officers were in command.

Other rank data are provided by Townsey (1982a) from information collected by the Police Foundation in 1979. For five cities, singled out by Townsey because they represent more progressive agencies, affirmative action wise, the percentage of white and black (in parentheses) women officers in 1979 were: Detroit 11.7% (7.5%); Washington, DC 7.3% (5.6%); Miami 6.2% (1.5%); Houston 6.1% (1.1%); and Denver 4.9% (0.9%).

In those same cities the women were almost all at the lowest rank. Here are the percentages of those white and black (again, in parentheses) women who held the *entry rank* of police officer: Detroit 84% (96%); Washington, DC 96% (98%); Miami 97% (100%); Houston 86% (98%); and Denver 72% (85%).

Salary

According to a 1985 survey by the International Personnel Management Association, police patrol officers had a median annual salary of about $21,700. They started at an average of $18,900 a year and could reach an average maximum of $25,100 a year (Bureau of Labor Statistics, 1988a).

Other figures *for both sexes* are median weekly earnings from the Department of Labor's *Monthly Labor Review* for 1986 of $478 or about $25,000 a year for "police and detectives, public service" (Mellor, 1987). The *Monthly Labor Review* is where one can pick up in timely news notes on salaries around the country, such as the fact that 1988 entry police salaries in Columbus, Ohio of $19,400 go to $32,000 in just three and half years, and that 1988 New York City salaries go from a base of $26,000 to $39,000 for rank-and-file officers.

Other overall, average annual salaries for law enforcement officers compiled by the Bureau of Justice for 1986 are $18,913 for a city police officer entry level, up to a $24,243 maximum, and $18,170 for a state trooper entry level, up to $28,033 maximum (Lindgren, 1988, p. 126).

It is hard to locate up-to-date figures for women because the Labor Department statisticians do not calculate median salaries for groups with fewer than 50,000 employees. But to provide some idea of how much women police make, overall, compared to men police, consider the median salaries for "protective services workers" (police officers and firefighters) in 1983. The median salary for white men was $24,200. While black and hispanic men got 93 percent and 98 percent of that $24,200, respectively, white women got 87 percent, hispanic women 89 percent, and black women 80 percent (Moss, 1988). Because police salaries, like other civil service salaries are closely tied to rank and years of service, the lower salaries for women reflect their concentration, as noted above, in the lower ranks, and their more recent entry into police work.

It is good to remember, however, that if a woman is being discriminated against in salary, the courts will not only order that her salary be brought up to the appropriate level, but that back pay be provided to compensate for the period during which she was underpaid. Potts (1983) illustrates this remediation with the case of a female deputy sheriff who was the only woman in a department with 13 male deputies. She had the same duties as all the other deputies, was third in seniority and fifth in the chain of command, but 15th in salary. The county in question was also told to desist from future sex discrimination in pay rates.

THE CONTINUING ISSUE:
WOMEN SPECIALISTS OR GENERALISTS?

This introductory chapter began with the story of how women entered policing through their specialist role. They kept this role for 50 years until the women's movement revived and civil rights legislation was enacted. A big issue from that point on has been shaking off the specialist role and being trained as generalists, just as men police are.

Men police have always been trained to be generalists first, and after they could do everything and had done everything, they could then specialize if they had the interest, skills, and motivation. Some men always preferred not to specialize but to remain generalist patrol officers throughout their careers.

Women, on the other hand, were given specialist duties and after they had perfected these duties, they continued to do them throughout their careers. The argument that nature and nurture especially equipped women for specialist roles was a product of the mores and thinking of the late 19th and early 20th centuries, just as the argument for equality which has replaced it is in line with late 20th century mores and thinking.

No one argues seriously today that there is no role for women in the police. People still do argue, however, as to whether that role should be specialist or generalist. Among police officers more women favor the generalist role for women than the specialist role. The opposite is probably true among men officers.

Men's Opinions

What position do men take who favor women in specialist positions? They used to use traditional arguments that women were *not* physically and emotionally strong enough for the seamy side of patrol, not courageous enough to shoot a gun, not big or awesome enough to deal with violent citizens. Traditional men probably still privately hold these opinions but in public prefer to reiterate that women possess *unique* skills in law enforcement, such as crime prevention, and say that there are still areas of police work "in which the best man for the job is . . . a woman" (Ullman, 1984). Specialist-believing administrators defend assigning certain functions to women on the grounds of efficiency and cost-effectiveness.

What position do men take who favor women as generalists? A chief advocate of this position is Peter Horne (1980, pp. 60–63). He says the male model of police work has always been to train a generalist. The model aimed for uniform training and for diversity in the product—an individual who had performed all aspects of police work including supervising when called upon in the field. Specialist roles came later.

So Horne asks, if this is the right model for a man, why not for a woman? If all officers are to identify with all the goals of an organization and to select their career paths only after they've had the opportunity to perform all police activities, then women must be utilized exactly as men are. If women with supervisory talent and training are to benefit the organization by eventually taking command, how can they, if they have not had the requisite, wide-ranging field experience? Thus, as Peter Horne does, generalist-believing administrators may well defend *not* channeling women into specialist roles on the grounds of efficiency and cost-effectiveness.

Horne (1980, p. 60) also observed some negative outcomes for administrators who follow the specialist philosophy. The first is that men officers resent it. Men feel that if women are to get equal pay, they should do equal work. Men feel that if men have to work their way up to specialist roles based on skills and productivity, then women should do the same. True, the men may argue that women can't do patrol work as well as men, and thus should not, but at the same time they resent it if women don't.

Women's Opinions

What position do women take who favor a specialist position? Probably they sound a bit old-fashioned as do men favoring specialization, but while men may privately still believe in specialization because of women's limitations, women favoring specialization argue on the basis of women's historic strengths.

Who better to mention than Lois Higgins, the first president of the reorganized (1956) International Association of Women Police and author of the *Policewoman's Manual* (1961)?

Throughout her *Manual* Ms. Higgins was definitely on the side of women's special work within the police. Women bring a "social viewpoint" to police work. She saw them doing patrol work but it was unique patrol work involving children and other women and emphasizing prevention.

She believed that women were here to stay in police work because of peculiarly feminine work talents, for example, a highly developed interest in human relationships. They were also here to stay because crime prevention as a major police function is now sufficiently accepted and supported.

What do the majority of women officers today who defend the generalist position have to say? Equal pay means equal work. They are ready to do all aspects of police work if the administration will only let them. They regard the men's resentment of women being given specialist positions as justified and see the only way to overcome this resentment is to be treated the same as men.

These generalists, "the new professionals," see themselves as law enforcement officers, not as social workers (Feinman, 1986, pp. 97–98). They want a career that offers a good salary and advancement. They want an integration of women into all aspects of law enforcement but they still retain traces of Alice Wells' and Mary Hamilton's prevention and protection mission, even as they fight to keep from being limited to women's traditional police roles.

Some Utilization Data

How is the specialist/generalist quarrel being translated into actual practice? Are women being over or under utilized in line with sex-role stereotypes and the specialist philosophy? Or are they being treated like the men? Research to date points to women being treated as generalists.

Townsey's (1982a) figures for the assignment of white and black women nationally in 1979 to seven different activities are as follows, white percentages first: patrol 61%, 63%; administrative 6%, 6%; investigative 10%, 7%; juvenile 11%, 11%; traffic 4%, 2%; technical 7%, 5%; and "other" 2%, 7%. The figures on patrol are gratifying, from a generalist perspective, as are the figures on juvenile and administrative services. It does not appear that women are being massively channeled away from basic line duty.

Garrison, Grant, and McCormick (1988) have more recent data on current utilization of women provided by 180 members of the International Association of Women Police. Inasmuch as they sent their one-page survey to 1,500 women, and the IAWP is a select group, the generalizability of these results could be questioned, but the data are worth considering.

Seventy-nine percent of this national sample had been in policing five years or more. Seventy-eight percent had worked in uniform patrol for a median time of 5 years. This fact seems to say, again, that the generalist philosophy dominates in practice. The next most frequent assignment was administrative services where 35 percent had experience, followed by tactical units in which 31 percent had experience, and "crimes against persons" where 19 percent had experience for a median time over 2 years. Only 12 percent had been assigned to juvenile work.

Individually, 47 percent of these women had had only one or no major assignment change. Eighty-two percent had had two or fewer major assignment changes. Surprisingly, number of assignments was not a function of years of service, which it should have been.

When on patrol 75 percent had worked in high crime locations and of these, 41 percent worked without a partner, 63 percent worked in a radio car, and only 2 percent worked day shift! It certainly doesn't appear that they were being given protected assignments.

Another recent study is that of Janus, Janus, Lord, and Power (1988). In their sample of 135 women officers, most from the New York City area, 67 percent were on patrol and 14 percent were detectives. Only 1 percent were in the youth division and only 2 percent in records. The remaining 16 percent were in the catchall "other" category. Again, we would have to say that the generalist philosophy is being practiced.

And even though some cities have been found to employ small percentages of women, such as Boston and Los Angeles with 4 percent in 1982, they may score very high in terms of the number of women on patrol. Boston had 58 of its 62 women doing patrol, or 94 percent, and Los Angeles had 210 of its 292 women doing patrol, or 72 percent. The worst city of the ten studied was Houston with 7 percent women in the department but only 32 percent of them on patrol (Linn and Price, 1985).

An Exemplary Utilization Study

A good objective way to investigate over or underutilization is to analyze official patrol car logs to see if women and men report the same activities to the same degree. This was the tack Snortum and Beyers (1983) took in the department in El Monte, a suburb of Los Angeles. They studied 26 new officers, 13 women and 13 men, with the same number of patrol shifts worked at the same hours, i.e., day-time, swing, and graveyard. Three blocks of duty (a year's worth) had been completed by six men and six women, two blocks (8 months) by ten men and ten women, and one block (4 months) by everyone, 13 men and 13 women. This gave Snortum and Beyers an average of 146 tours of duty per officer and *2,773 recorded incidents per officer* for comparison. A lot of data.

Eight broad categories of patrol activities were analyzed: station detail such as desk and dispatcher relief; traffic stops; pedestrian stops; vehicle stops for questioning and search; "other observations" meaning location and bar checks; high risk calls for in-progress burglary, murder, etc.; disturbance calls for fights and quarrels; and last, "other radio calls" for auto and petty theft. The last three activities were assigned by a dispatcher.

and the other categories of activities were self-initiated, except, of course, station detail.

In all those data, Snortum and Beyers found only two differences between the sexes. The first was that during the first block of duty men were dispatched to more high risk calls than the women, but this difference disappeared for officers who worked for longer periods. The other difference occurred in the second and third blocks of duty for "station detail." To see if women were perhaps being diverted to sex-role stereotyped activities such as clerical tasks in the station, Snortum and Beyers looked at 70 specific activities in the eight categories of activity, looking for under and overutilization of women.

These investigators defined "overutilization" as an activity in which the women did at least 10 percent more than expected, and underutilization meant they did 10 percent less than expected. The activity which showed the greatest overutilization was prisoner search. This was because men prisoners were searched by a male jailer but there was no female jailer in this small town. So prisoner search seems a justified example of overutilization. Snortum and Beyers regard the other overutilized categories as also appropriate—rape, found child, indecent exposure, and child abuse. It turned out that the women served *less* than their fair share of dispatcher relief and desk officer relief, so they were not being singled out for clerical work.

Perhaps the best finding was that there was no activity in which the women were being *underutilized.* There were no significant differences on any of the four major areas of self-initiated patrol activity: traffic stops, pedestrian checks, vehicle stops, and "other observations." And these young officers were *really* working. Snortum and Beyers compare their 14 incidents per tour for one-man cars and 12 incidents per tour for one-woman cars with incident per tour rates in Washington, DC of 5 for men and 4 for women. They also cite Washington, DC's crimes per officer in 1976 as 12 crimes per officer whereas the rate in El Monte in 1976 was 66 crimes per officer. The authors tease that they could make the case that the El Monte women could work circles around the Washington, DC men. But, in all seriousness, they say that no matter what pace men officers set, women can approximate it.

THE PROSPECTS

As mentioned earlier in this chapter, the percent growth expected between 1986 and the year 2000 in police officers is 17 percent. The Bureau of Labor Statistics bulletin (1988b) which reports this fact also compared patrol officers and police detectives with other occupations on a number of critical employment variables. The number of rank and file police officers who will be employed, comparatively speaking, is going to be "very high." Median weekly earnings will be comparatively "high." Their separation rate will be "very low," as will their unemployment rate. The report also reminds us that police officers are principally "trained by their employer" and through post-secondary college courses, but that a bachelor's degree is not required (p. 10).

These are projections to pay attention to. They portend an area of career opportunity, especially for women. Policing is also an area of challenge and responsibility, of change and adaptability. What follows is an attempt to make that career come alive, not by exaggerating aspects of the job that occur very infrequently, nor by understating its stresses and difficulties. What follows is the reality of women police today as reported by social scientists, police experts, and, yes, newspaper journalists such as Tom Seligman.

Chapter 2

PERSPECTIVES ON 1970s RESEARCH

66 S hould Women Be On The Patrol Force?" is the title of a table in
Peter Bloch, Deborah Anderson, and Pamela Gervais (1973), probably the most referenced evaluation study of the 1970s. This title aptly
depicts what that research was all about—women's competence on patrol.

The table gives the percentages of various members of the Washington,
DC police community who answered in the affirmative. Here are those
groups with the percentage saying "yes": white women officers, 93 percent; black women officers, 79 percent; black men officers, 67 percent;
white men officers, 32 percent; sergeants, 32 percent; and captains and
lieutenants, 22 percent. This is the sort of finding the 1970s' evaluation
studies reported.

Before taking up the content of these studies, however, first some
comments on who does research on women police and where it can be
found.

The people who did research on women in the 1970s, typically, were
professional evaluation researchers such as Bloch, Anderson, and Gervais.
For these researchers, evaluation is their job; they conduct social science
research projects to make a living. They do not pick the topics they
pursue; topics are dictated by the organizations using their services.
However, while these organizations might wish the results to turn out
one way or the other, evaluation researchers are usually objective, unbiased,
fair, reputable professionals. (The bias of organizations, however, does
enter into the sorts of items they give researchers to evaluate.)

Research by professional evaluators has given way in the 1980s to
research by law enforcement, criminal justice, and *police science academicians* and their graduate students. For this group, research is also part of
the job. They do studies about women police in order to publish rather
than perish. They may or may not be prowomen in policing. Academicians simply have to have a research area to make their mark in, and, for
some, women police just happens to be it.

Last, *prowomen and feminist scholars* are beginning to do research on women police. For this group the particular topics they choose to research are very important. And while findings are treated objectively and unbiasedly, results are often interpreted from a woman's point of view. Feminist researchers typically acknowledge their bias, however, while other scholars typically do not.

Another way in which research on women police is changing is *where* that literature is to be found. Less and less of it is published as technical reports emanating from police organizations. More and more such research is appearing in scholarly journals, the major one of which is the *Journal of Police Science and Administration* published by the International Association of Chiefs of Police in Gaithersburg, Maryland. Another journal is *Police Studies* edited at John Jay College of Criminal Justice, City University of New York.

Studies about women police also appear in professional magazines. *WomenPolice* is published by the International Association of Women Police, Dayton, Ohio. *Police Chief* is published by the International Association of Chiefs of Police in Gaithersburg, Md. There are also *Law and Order* and the *FBI Law Enforcement Bulletin.*

More mention of women police is being made today in criminal justice textbooks. Whereas women used to be treated in a few paragraphs in such tomes, now they may deserve an entire chapter such as "The Evolving Role of Women in American Policing" by Linn and Price which appears in Abraham Blumberg and Elaine Niederhoffer's (1985) *The Ambivalent Force* (3rd edition). Similarly, Imogene Moyer's (1985) *The Changing Roles of Women in the Criminal Justice System* includes a chapter on "Women in Police Academy Training" by Diane Pike.

And last, there are popular books written about women police such as Bryna Taubman's *Lady Cop* (1987) based on interviews with women in New York City and Molly Martin's *Hard-Hatted Women* (1988) which includes an interview with a San Francisco woman police officer.

THE MAJOR CONCERN:
WOMEN'S COMPETENCE ON PATROL

Actually, there were not that many evaluation studies in the 1970s. People speak of seven to nine "major" ones. But they were done on a grand scale, as applied research studies go, by professional social scientists for large police organizations, sometimes with outside funding from auspices such as the Police Foundation in Washington, DC.

The evaluators were trying to answer the concerns of these big organizations with respect to women's behavior as police officers compared to men's behavior. One way to judge what was important in the hundreds of pages of reports that were produced is to look at what experts have said about their results.

Expert Opinions of the Evaluation Studies

Daniel Bell (1982) is sympathetic to women in policing. He looked at three aspects to the evaluation studies: what they found regarding women's competence, what they found as far as citizen reactions to women police were concerned, and what they found about male colleagues' attitudes.

Bell summed up the competence studies by saying they demonstrated that women were generally equal to male officers. He also noted minor sex differences which showed up from study to study, such as finding that women officers made fewer arrests and that men were perceived as better at handling violent confrontations.

Bell said the citizen reaction studies demonstrated that citizens favored women over men police. Typically, citizens were neutral or approving of the assignment of women to patrol. But, also, women received fewer complaints and more compliments from the public.

All of the studies Bell reviewed on men officers' attitudes toward women officers found those attitudes to be negative. For example, he reported that male officers thought women made their jobs more difficult because the men had to protect the women and couldn't expect to be backed up by them. Black officers were more favorable toward women police than whites. Bell concluded that the main obstacle for women entering the police was not lack of competence or lack of citizen support, but discrimination from within the police organization.

Lawrence Sherman (1985) is one of the country's outstanding academicians interested in women police, and he, too, is sympathetic toward women in policing. He summed up the evaluation studies differently than Bell, concentrating strictly on competence. He divided police behavior into four activities. *Detection* activities are decisions to take crime reports from complainants and to stop and question people. *Arrest* activities refer to deciding to arrest. *Service* activities include the manner in which officers settle disputes and interact with citizens. *Violence* activities are the justified and unjustified use of any physical force against citizens.

Sherman wanted to see if individual characteristics such as age, race, and sex of officer were related to the findings of the 1970s' studies using these four classifications of police behavior. He concluded that there was no relationship between sex and the findings for service activities. He concluded that were no data on which to base findings between sex and violent behaviors. And as far as the studies of both detection activities and arrest activities were concerned, the studies' findings were "mixed," such as some studies finding women made fewer arrests than men, and other studies finding their arrests records were the same as men's. Sherman's analysis leaves one feeling that the studies lacked conclusiveness.

Peter Horne (1980), an advocate of women in all areas of policing, used the 1970s' Washington, DC study as a standard against which to compare six other evaluations. Three of them, he found, had findings similar the DC study, the other three were less decisive.

Of the DC evaluation Horne said that in addition to finding that men and women performed patrol work in a similar manner and that there was no reason to doubt that women could do it satisfactorily, the public was very positive toward the women. The women officers, further, were more effective than patrolmen in defusing potentially violent situations. The women fostered a less aggressive style of policing and were less likely to exhibit unbecoming conduct (p. 101).

Horne says the St. Louis County evaluation had parallel results. The women did patrol duties equally well as men, had a less aggressive style, and were equally effective in managing distraught citizens. St. Louis citizens rated the women high on sensitivity to human needs. Horne notes that St. Louis County uses one-officer vehicles so that this was a particularly good test of women's ability to handle hazardous calls (p. 102).

Another report with findings like those in DC, Horne states, was that done for the New York City Police Department. Here, male and female officers performed similarly, used the same techniques, and were equally likely to use force and weapons (p. 103).

Regarding the Denver Police Department study, Horne emphasized the lack of difference in performance between women and men in all aspects of police work from number of arrests and effects of officers on levels of violence, to injuries, efficiency ratings, and written reports. The report also said that men had more citizens' complaints and double the rate of resistance to arrest women received (p. 103).

The other three evaluations were less laudatory toward women officers. The California State patrol study showed women could satisfactorily perform the duties of a state traffic officer, but that it cost more to recruit, train, and maintain them than men (p. 102). The Pennsylvania State trooper study found that some women were able to perform most trooper duties, but wasn't more definitive (p. 101). And, of the Philadelphia Police Department's commissioned research, Horne says they set out to prove that women couldn't do the job and consequently concluded that they could not perform beat patrol as safely and efficiently as men. The report based this finding primarily on two factors, one, that men were rated higher than women in handling building searches, and two, that men projected strength and power more than women. The federal judge who made the final ruling on the discrimination case which led to the Philadelphia study did not accept the report and ordered Philadelphia to cease discriminating against women (p. 104).

Horne's final summary is that the "results are in, and the facts are there. Policewomen can do the job on patrol (p. 105)."

EVALUATING THE EVALUATION STUDIES

Merry Morash and Jack Greene (1986), professors of criminal justice, she at Michigan State, he at Temple University, belong to that growing group of academic researchers on women police.

They have provided us with an *empirical* review of the famous and infamous evaluation studies of the 1970s. They accomplished this by getting nine female and male upper-level criminal justice undergraduates to participate in an evaluation study of the evaluation studies.

The nine studies the students rated and judged were done in the 1970s in Pennsylvania, Washington, DC, St. Louis, California, Denver, Newton, Massachusetts, New York City, and Philadelphia (2 studies).

These nine studies focused on women's performance compared to men's as police officers. Only the second Philadelphia study concluded that women were not as capable as males. All the other studies found that the sexes were equally capable.

While the studies concluded women on patrol were as capable as men, the studies also all found small differences, as Bell (1982) noted in his review. If researchers do hundreds of comparisons, they are bound to find small differences which they may or may not be able to replicate. These little differences shouldn't be taken too seriously, but they are food for thought for police administrators, and the rest of us. Here are some of the slight differences between the sexes Morash and Greene chose to report from the nine studies.

Women weren't as good with firearms and had more accidents. Women had higher attrition rates and more costly injuries. Women made fewer arrests and traffic stops and issued fewer citations. Women's partners made more decisions and gave more instructions out in the field and did more necessary strenuous activity. On the other hand, women had a less aggressive style of policing and were viewed more favorably by the public. Women were less frequently charged with serious misconduct, they received fewer citizen complaints, and they met with less resistance.

When Morash and Greene added up all the individual questions or items included in the nine studies, there was a grand total of 2,194 items for analysis. These came from a wide variety of data-gathering instruments. Surveys — of police officers, supervisors, victims, citizens. Records — from police academies and departmental files. Rating schedules used by observers to code and judge behaviors they saw for themselves.

The nine coders Morash and Greene trained made eight kinds of judgments about each of the 2,194 items: (1) Was the item related to a male stereotype? (2) What was that male stereotype? (3) Was the item related to a female stereotype? (4) What was that female stereotype? (5) Was the item related to a police performance behavior? (6) What was the police performance behavior? (7) Did the item specify a particular crime or incident? (8) What was the crime or incident the item specified?

As can be seen, Morash and Greene were interested in three aspects to the items. Were the items measuring conformity to a male or female stereotype? Did the items measure identifiable police performance behaviors? Were the tasks the police were performing, in fact, related to a particular crime or incident?

Regarding the existence of gender stereotypes among the items, nearly 1 out of 10 items were found to refer to stereotypes, the ratio of male stereotypes to female stereotypes being five to one. What were the male stereotypes looked for? Forceful, dominant, acting like a leader, athletic, aggressive. Only 31 items referred to female stereotypes. "Gentle" and "understanding" accounted for 24 of the 31.

These results suggest that a substantial number of items on which the women officers were evaluated had little to do with police work. The items simply represented attributes commonly associated with "men's work." Such items obviously put women at a disadvantage.

To what extent did the items refer to identifiable police performance behaviors? Readers may find this hard to believe, but only 47 percent of the 2,194 items were judged to refer to police activities. The eight types of activities were: patrol, citizen contact, traffic, community and public relations, reporting, weapons, physical activities and use of force, and "other." The police organizations varied wildly in how many items had to do with performance. Only 24 percent of Newton, Mass's items referred to police performance and only 28 percent of St. Louis's. In contrast, Philadelphia's two studies referred to police performance behaviors in 79 percent and 100 percent of their items respectively.

So it is important to remember that 53 percent of the items on which these women police were evaluated had nothing to do with job performance.

Overall, 32 percent of the job performance behaviors were considered "patrol" and another 32 percent "citizen contact" behaviors. Both of these figures seem reasonable. But some other figures make no sense at all. For example, overall only 0.6 percent of behaviors were "community and public relations," and only 0.8 percent were in the "other" category, which included activities such as processing evidence, filling out forms, collecting fines, and lockup responsibilities! How can community and public relations represent less than one percent of officers' activities? At the same time, how can St. Louis' officers engage in 36 percent "weapons activities" and New York police in 44 percent "physical exertion activities?"

How do Morash and Greene explain such unlikely results? They say that the studies inadequately sampled the police work environment. The studies deemphasized required and frequent behaviors disliked by the police, and overemphasized activities that reflect wishful thinking along male stereotypical lines. But when an evaluation instrument does not accurately reflect the true, mundane nature of police work, how can such a measure fairly evaluate anyone's performance?

The last of the judgments the coders made had to do with whether or not items mentioned a specific crime or incident. Only 23 percent of items in fact did so! In New York City only 4 percent of the items mentioned a particular crime or incident. The high for mentioning crimes was 59 percent of items in one of the Philadelphia studies.

The problem with *not* specifying a particular type of crime or incident for 77 percent of the tasks is that it tempts us to think that what held for the tasks where incidents were mentioned, holds for the other 77 percent of unspecified tasks as well. But did it? There's no way to know.

Looking at the 23 percent crime-specified items, that is, the 508 items that referred to a crime or incident, the coders classified them as follows: violent crimes, 11 percent; violent order-maintenance situations, 55 percent; nonviolent crimes, 17 percent; nonviolent order-maintenance situations, 17 percent.

These last figures illustrate yet another way in which the women police evaluated by these instruments in the 1970s were not evaluated fairly. They lead one to believe that two-thirds of incidents are violent, when, in fact, the bulk of police work consists of nonviolent and service activities. Further, the items compare women and men on an artificial standard, that is, the ability to deal with constant violent and confrontative behavior.

Morash and Greene remind us that in Philadelphia Study 1, avoiding arrest was positively evaluated, but Philadelphia Study 2, a high number of arrests was positively evaluated. In Study 1, calling for backup was positively assessed, but in Study 2, it was negatively assessed. Study 1 concluded that women were as good as, if not better in their performance than men, whereas Study 2 concluded women were less cost effective.

This valuable evaluation of the evaluations brings us face to face with the issue of what *tasks* are most important to police work—infrequent, atypical critical events, such as subduing an armed felon? Or frequent, typical tasks such as talking to citizens and routine patrolling that take up most of an officer's time? It also brings us face to face with the issue of what *goals* a police service is trying to achieve, and how tasks contribute positively or negatively to achieving goals. For example, is "better" police performance many arrests, or few arrests? Calling for backup, or not having to call for backup? Using understanding and gentleness or force and aggression?

THE PROTOTYPIC STUDY OF THE 1970S

Here is a more detailed look at the Washington, DC study of "Police-women on Patrol" as reported by Bloch, Anderson, and Gervais in 1973, and by Bloch and Anderson in 1974. It represents one of the best pieces of research on women police, so it serves as a model for the other studies reviewed in this book.

It is a rich study, suggesting myriad ways police behavior can be measured. The small but fascinating differences between the women and men are filled with provocative suggestions for further research. While the two reports, indeed, address women's competence, they just as powerfully document men's enormous resistance. They turned out to be as much about men's attitudes as they were about women's behavior.

Rather than assess or critique the Washington, DC study, I am going to use it to sensitize readers to the multitude of conclusions that can be reached, based on any one study. This presentation is intended to under-score the advice that, in the last analysis, everyone should probably read research reports in the original. Every reviewer, every referencer, gets out of a piece of research what he or she wants to, and wishes to pass on to other people. Depending on mental set, one can reach totally opposite conclusions based on the same carefully conducted, empirical study.

First, I will present ten results a reader biased *against* women on patrol might choose to remember. Then I will recount ten results a reader *positive* toward women on patrol might take away from the same report. Then I ask readers, what do *you* think?

First, the First Report on "Policewomen on Patrol" of 1973 based on the first four months of the project and on the experiences of 80 new women officers and 80 new men officers. What would a reader who read the report through a *filter negative toward women* say the report found?

An antiwomen reader might remember the following:

1. Before women were assigned to patrol, only one official thought they would make his job easier. Ninety-two percent of officials said their jobs would be more difficult.

2. Women officers made fewer misdemeanor arrests and gave fewer moving traffic violations than the men, and only 47 percent of the women made one or more felony arrests, compared to 61 percent of the men.

3. Observers found male-female teams less likely than male-male teams to initiate traffic or non-traffic incidents.

4. Observers found new women were more likely than new men to be given instructions by their senior partner and were less likely to take charge at incidents where their partner was present.

5. Only 68 percent of the new women had passed the Department's driving test by a certain date compared to 88 percent of the new men.

6. Men and women officers and officials all agreed that fewer women than men with a year's street experience could handle down and out drunks, disorderly males, and threatening situations where someone had a knife or gun.

7. New women received 63 complaints versus only one for new men on the Chief's departmental survey.

8. More women (68 percent) than men (39 percent) took *some* sick leave.

9. Both women and men on patrol and officials preferred male partners (48 percent of women and 31 percent of men officers had no preference).

10. Men officers where women were assigned were *less favorable* about women's abilities than men in districts with no women.

Now, what about a reader biased *in favor of women* on patrol. What are some of the report's conclusions this person would make note of?

1. *All* of the new women compared to 94 percent of the new men were rated as likely to be recommended for retention at the end of one year.

2. With a 4 point rating as "average," new women were rated slightly less capable (4.43) than new men (4.87) on the Chief's departmental survey by district commanders.

3. On this same survey commanders judged women to be men's equals on the specific abilities of dealing with the public, handling a disorderly female, handling an accident, and making a crime report.

4. There were no differences in the performance of new women and new men in the few situations they encountered involving violence or potential violence.

5. Forty-six percent of citizens approved of women on patrol, 23 percent were neutral, and 31 percent disapproved.

6. Citizens thought a woman and a man working as a team had a slight advantage over an all-male team in handling fights between women and men.

7. Citizens felt women officers would show slightly more respect for citizens and receive slightly more respect from citizens.

8. In a patrol survey, men officers "consistently and strikingly" indicated a less favorable response from the public than did women. The men felt the public was less cooperative, and they reported receiving 50 percent more insults, close to three times as many threats or attempts at injury, and less than half the number of compliments than women reported.

9. The total number of days of sick leave used by the men and women was the same.

10. Men and women officers and officials agree women are better than men at questioning rape victims.

Now for the Final Report on "Policewomen on Patrol" (1974) based on 86 new women officers and 86 new men officers over a period of one year.

The reader *biased against women* on patrol might remember the following:

1. Men handled more patrol incidents per tour than women, primarily because they wrote more traffic citations.

2. Men also made more felony arrests, misdemeanor arrests, and moving traffic citations than women.

3. Citizens gave women officers lower ratings than men officers in dealing with people who were dangerous, angry or upset.

4. On the Chief's Survey commanders rated the patrol abilities of women as poorer than men on general performance, protecting a partner from violence, handling a public fight, and handling disorderly males.

5. On the Officials' Survey Ratings women were rated as less competent than men on general patrol competence, ability to handle domestic fights, and ability to handle street violence.

6. Women needed two weeks longer than men to pass the driving test.

7. Police officials agreed with men officers that women officers were not as likely to be as satisfactory as men in several types of violent situations.

8. Men officers had a definite preference for patrolling with a male partner.

9. Men officers doubted women officers were the equal of men in most patrol skills and there was little change in their attitudes from the start to the end of the project.

10. Men who worked with women were more negative toward them than men who had not worked with women.

In contrast, the reader *in favor of women* on patrol could cite these findings:

1. Arrests made by new women and new men were equally likely to result in convictions.

2. New women worked as well as new men with senior partners, sharing driving about equally, taking charge with about the same frequency, and giving instructions about equally.

3. Performance ratings indicated equal overall satisfaction with officers of both sexes. There were no statistically significant differences between women and men in first year performance Departmental ratings overall, or in the specific categories of bearing and behavior, human relations, learning ability, knowledge and skill, acceptance of responsibility, written expression, oral expression, and performance of duty.

4. There was no difference between the women and men in number of sick days used.

5. There was no difference between the women and men in number of injuries sustained or number of days absent from work due to injuries.

6. There was no difference between the women and men in the number of driving accidents.

7. Women were less likely than the men to have been charged with serious unbecoming conduct.

8. Similar numbers of new women (12) and new men (11) resigned.

9. Citizens who had observed women officers in action said they had become somewhat more favorably inclined toward women officers.

10. Police officials agreed with women officers that women and men were equally able to handle the important patrol situations of settling family disputes, getting information at crime scenes, handling disorderly females, cruising around and observing, and handling traffic accidents.

If you had been a police administrator, after digesting the above, what would your reaction have been? Most police agencies, upon reading the two reports by Bloch and his colleagues, accepted that women could perform the job of patrol. And that they had better get on with a policy of no sex discrimination in the hiring of police officers. For example, Madison, Wisconsin, wanting to avoid being compelled by another authority to adopt a non-discriminatory policy, held in-service training classes led by a female detective and male captain to identify problems and come up with solutions. Then several officers were sent to inspect the women-on-patrol programs in New York City and Washington, DC. Subsequently, recruitment was redesigned to bring in a large group of women to counteract isolation and training was altered to provide karate for the women (Milton et al., 1974). How many other departments across the country responded as Madison did, we do not know, but the Washington, DC evaluation study was a great impetus for change.

RESEARCH EXPECTATIONS OF THE 1980S

Peter Horne's (1980) second edition of *Women in Law Enforcement* was the most comprehensive book about women police at the start of this decade. It was directed at police administrators; it was aimed at increasing the numbers of women in the police service.

As one of the most knowledgeable and far-sighted experts on women police officers, Horne also saw the need for various kinds of studies in the 1980s. What did he suggest needed doing? What goals for research did he prescribe? What did he hope would get done?

Horne was most concerned that not enough experimentation had been done on *where best to utilize women officers.* He genuinely felt that only if police administrators experimented with women in different capacities would they achieve maximum efficiency from their personnel. Even though he felt the evaluation studies had been very good, he said much more needed to be done. He opined that many more definitive studies were needed before women gained full equality in law enforcement (p. 195).

Horne's book touched on many topics related to the full integration of women into the field and presumably he felt all were worthy topics for research. Absenteeism and turnover. How to handle pregnancy. The question of part-time work for trained women raising families. Stress. Family support or lack of support. Teamwork between women and men. Men's attitudes and resistance. The impact of women on the traditional thinking of police agencies. The modern shift to prevention. The question of women's style arousing less antagonism and provoking less violence. Is policing changing women or are women changing policing, or both? Is the future of policing androgynous officers with the best characteristics of both sexes? How have traditional policies and values been reassessed since the influx of women, policies regarding stature, agility, physical training, physical fitness, firearms training?

Horne had high hopes for research on women police in the 1980s. Now is the time to see how closely his vision and expectations were matched by the studies that were undertaken.

Chapter 3

BACKGROUND, FAMILY, AND LIFESTYLES

What are the backgrounds of women police? Their parents' occupations? Present family life? Recreational interests? Lifestyles?

Cristina Murphy, a 27-year-old divorced patrol officer with the Rochester, New York Police Department is white, dark-haired, soft-spoken. Off-duty she's like everyone's "sweet kid cousin," to be found at home in jeans and a peasant blouse. Mornings in her apartment she does housework and cooks. Her father was a lithographer, her mother a school teacher. She majored in Spanish in college and her home is filled with books and paintings and a parrot who doesn't talk. She's been a champion shooter in the New York State Police Olympics. She's got a police officer boyfriend who is sweet, bright, warm, and goodlooking. Their dates are at very odd hours because Murphy works the 2:45 p.m. to 11 p.m. shift, crazy hours which make having a family impossible. So she's thinking of quitting patrol and doing juvenile work. She's recognized by the guys as very good with kids, even though she doesn't have any of her own, and many of them do. She'd like to get married and have a family, but she'd also like to make captain. One woman's background, family situation, and lifestyle. Part of the description Claudia Dreifus wrote for *Police Magazine* in 1980.

Ten years later in Seattle, Washington. Police officer Marsha Wilson, black, age 36, and "not the world's greatest conversationalist," described to a newspaper reporter how she grew up in Baltimore in a household of two burglar uncles and a mother and grandmother who were maids. Wilson studied photography at the Rochester Institute of Technology, and to repay college loans enlisted in the Army. She attended Army photography school and was in the Army eight years, working for the Army Security Agency, a branch of the National Security Agency in Virginia and later in Germany. She studied offset printing after the Army but decided to try police work because she enjoyed the order and discipline of Army life. Her duties as an evidence specialist are to process crime scenes, taking fingerprints, blood and hair samples, and

33

photographs. Her strengths for police work, besides her technical skills, are that she's able to remain calm and to genuinely enjoy interacting with people of different backgrounds, beliefs, and cultures (Gelernter, 1989).

The trouble is that most of what is known about the background of women police is written at this level, that is, the level of the case study, the single interviewee, the anecdote. *The background* of women officers is probably the least researched topic reported here.

Which made this a difficult chapter to write. What we have are glimpses, very partial data. We will come away from it still knowing next to nothing about women officers' politics, religion, favorite spectator sports, tastes in art and music, how they spend their spare time, how they spend their money. The two most glaring omissions, from a social scientist's view, however, are their families' socioeconomic status, and the proportions who grew up in rural, suburban, and urban settings.

At this point in time the demographic profile of women police officers remains largely unknown. What follows is only a sketch of what is, undoubtedly, an engaging, complex, and colorful portrait.

BACKGROUND CHARACTERISTICS

In her brief history of women in law enforcement, Clarice Feinman (1986, p. 84) used New York City as a case study of what it used to take to become a policewoman.

Women reformers after WWI persuaded the New York state legislature to pass a law to establish the position of policewoman permanently in New York City. In 1921 twenty-five women who had passed the first civil service examination for policewomen completed training and went forth from the Women's Precinct stationhouse on 34th Street to gather up wayward women and neglected children.

Requirements stipulated that they be U. S. citizens between 21 and 35 years of age, have a high school diploma, and pass written, oral, and physical examinations. Experience in probation work, teaching, or nursing was desirable. They were to focus their duties on moral protection and prevention of delinquency. In contrast, men police at that time were not required to have any sort of education or work experience or focus to their jobs.

These first twenty-five women were all white and middle or upper class, most were married, many were college graduates, and most had

had careers in social work, probation, or education. They were active in social reform organizations and it is not surprising that the commissioner of police expected that they would not only save women and children but raise the morals and standards of the whole department as well (p. 87).

Women police have come a long way from the requirements of the 1920s and, perhaps, a long way from these descriptions of the first women in the service. To what extent does this early profile still fit today's women in terms of race, education, and previous work experience?

Race

A big difference from the 1920s that we would reasonably expect is that not all women police would be white. The argument for bringing minorities into the police service is the same as it is for bringing in women— that the organization can serve the community better to the degree that it represents that community. The 1990s demand that the police service no longer reflect racist and sexist thinking.

Consequently, one might think that the racial composition of police departments across this country would vary greatly, reflecting the wide variation in percentage of nonwhites in our cities, which in 1981 was: Washington, DC, 73 percent; Oakland, 61 percent; Cleveland, 46 percent; Kansas City, 29 percent; Oklahoma City, 20 percent (Hochstedler, Regoli, and Poole, 1984). But, as a rule, the percentage of nonwhites, especially the percentage of blacks, is well below their proportions in the general population. In 1981, Hochstedler et al. say blacks were 48 percent sworn personnel in Washington, DC, 22 percent in Oakland, 16 percent in Cleveland, 17 percent in Kansas City, and in Oklahoma City, 5 percent.

And it was the same for the groups of women police who participated in the studies reported here. While women may number ten percent of the sworn force in a given department, usually over 80 percent of that ten percent is white.

For example, of the 180 IAWP members who answered Garrison, Grant, and McCormick's (1988) survey, 89 percent were white, 6 percent black, and 3 percent Hispanic. Among the 68 women studied by Hunt, McCadden, and Mordaunt (1983) 18 percent were black. Weisheit's (1987) sample of 42 female Illinois State Troopers was 91 percent white. Of the 20 women Meagher and Yentes (1986) surveyed, only 3 (15 percent) were black. And of the 34 women working for an unidentified department in

1977, 6 percent were black and 6 percent were American Indian or Asian American (Hoffman, Little, and Perlstein, 1980). It certainly appears that black women continue to be underrepresented in the police service.

Education

Women police are often believed to be more educated than men police, perhaps as a holdover from the days when they had to have high school diplomas or even a college education, whereas men had no educational requirement. Certainly, one of the most important descriptors for Garrison, Grant, and McCormick's (1988) national sample of women police was their high educational level. Less than 6 percent had only a high school education. Seventy-one percent had completed some or all of a college education, and 23 percent had done post-graduate work or had terminal degrees.

The same high educational level characterized the 135 women studied by Janus, Janus, Lord, and Power (1988). Nine percent were high school graduates, 56 percent had some college education, 24 percent had bachelor's degrees, and eleven percent were pursuing or had completed graduate work.

Perhaps because they were university police officers, the five women interviewed by James Ferrier (1985) either had bachelor's degrees or were earning them while employed. All three with degrees had a B. S. in criminal justice. One with an associate of arts degree in law enforcement was pursuing a nursing degree. Their emergency medical technician skills were emphasized by Ferrier; they all excelled as EMTs.

And at the end of this chapter, in presenting background differences from male colleagues, the evidence, again, is that women tend to be more educated. It is my prediction, however, that education is a difference between the sexes which may well disappear over the next decade with greater numbers of women in the police. I would expect educational level to continue to be different from one department and agency to another, but within agencies, for women and men not to differ in years of schooling.

Previous Work Experience

Of the 28 women officers she studied Martin (1980) said that there was little in their work histories to lead them to choose a nontraditional occupation. Of the twenty-two with prior work experience, only three had done anything such as bus driving, that might be considered nontraditional. Almost all had held low level clerical and sales jobs (p. 61).

Perhaps the best data available on the previous jobs of women police officers have been provided by Donald Zytowski (1989) who requested as part of his Kuder interest inventory study what other occupations the women had held. These 348 women listed a total of 609 previous jobs, excluding military service and student status.

I looked separately at the jobs listed by the 190 women satisfied to be police officers, the 116 women "slightly dissatisfied" with policing, and the 42 women (12 percent) who would choose a different occupation if they were starting over again. I coded each job by interest area and level of education required.

Their previous jobs fell in all eight interest groups: Service, Business Contact (persuasive selling), Organization, Technical, Outdoor, Scientific, General Cultural, and Arts & Entertainment. Jobs were also coded into three educational levels: high school diploma alone required; college or technical training required beyond high school diploma but no college degree required; college degree or higher required.

Had these three job satisfaction groups come to police work from different interest groups? Had they previously worked at different levels before entering the police? "Not obviously" is the answer to both questions.

The interest area 40 percent of them came from was "Organization," and the jobs most frequently held in the Organizational area were dispatcher, office clerk, secretary, retail sales clerk, and cashier. As you can see, only the job of secretary requires much training beyond a high school diploma.

Roughly 30 percent of the women had previously held "Service" jobs, the interest group to which not only counselors and social workers, bartenders and barbers belong, but also police and firefighters, in this interest coding scheme. While a few of the women had been jailers, probation officers, and caseworkers, the law enforcement job most frequently listed was security guard. Far more of them, however, had been waitresses. Again, as with the Organizational jobs, most had been working in the Service area at very low levels for which only minimal training was necessary.

Negligible numbers of the women had been employed in the "Business Contact" area which involves direct, persuasive selling. Likewise very few had held Arts & Entertainment, Outdoor, or Scientific jobs. This leaves two areas, Technical jobs and General Cultural jobs. Roughly 8 percent had held technical jobs, most at the lowest level, on assembly lines and in factories. Another 8 percent had come from the General Cultural area and only here had women left high level occupations for the police. Teaching was the most frequently mentioned job in the General Cultural area, but among these police officers were also former journalists, librarians, editors, and attorneys, also considered "General Cultural" occupations.

Looking at previous job level, 54 percent had come from jobs that required only a high school education. Thirty-three percent had come from jobs that required education beyond high school but not a college degree, as does the job of police officer. Only 13 percent listed previous jobs that required a college degree or beyond.

How many jobs had they previously held? Eight percent had had no previous jobs, one-third one previous job, and a quarter two previous jobs. Seventeen percent had had three previous jobs, 8 percent four jobs, 6 percent five jobs, and 3 percent more than five jobs.

The "previous work experience" of women police today is thus very different from that of women in the first half of this century. As many women now come from organizational jobs as from social service jobs, and many, many more come from low level jobs than from professions requiring college degrees.

PRESENT FAMILY STATUS

Most of the women Clarice Feinman (1986) described in New York City in the 1920s were married. Is this true today?

Marital Status

The answer to that question is a resounding "no." In fact, women police appear to be *less married* than other women. For example . . .

Garrison, Grant, and McCormick's (1988) sample of 180 IAWP members who responded to a survey about how they were being utilized were: single 58 percent, married 33 percent, divorced and widowed 9 percent. Most had no children (62 percent) and newer officers were the least likely to have children.

Janus, Janus, Lord, and Power's (1988) sample of 135 women police, all with rank below lieutenant, were: single 39 percent, married 28 percent, divorced 24 percent, and separated or widowed 9 percent. Sixty-one percent had no children, a figure extremely close to that found among IAWPers.

Wexler and Logan (1983) interviewed 25 women in depth who worked for a large, metropolitan police department in California. They say they deliberately chose persons so that different races, lengths of service, stations, and sexual preferences would be represented. Twenty percent (5) of the women were married or in an exclusive heterosexual relationship, twenty-four percent (6) of the women were homosexual, and 56 percent or 14 of the women were single and dating men.

And, last, of Susan Martin's (1980) 27 male officers, 11 were currently married, while 8, or 29 percent, of her 28 women officers were married.

Being "less married," however, does not mean no conflict over marriage and family. Cristina Murphy's quandary is fairly common among women officers.

Cops Marrying Cops

One of the biggest sex differences in Marlies Ott's (1989) research on Dutch police officers was that 65 percent of the women dated, lived with, or were married to colleagues, whereas this was true for only 8 percent of the men.

We don't have national statistics on marriages between U. S. police officers, but a recent article reported 50 police marriages in the 2,300 member Dallas Police Department and said that the trend would continue nationwide because of "propinquity," that is, the tendency to be attracted to people we're near (Chance, 1988). Thus, as more and more women go into police work, there are going to be a lot more cops marrying cops.

What did Sue Chance learn about police marriages from the five couples she interviewed? They reported many advantages to marrying another police officer. They helped one another maintain non-police friendships and avoid the clannishness typical of police. They helped one another get promoted. One man had been on patrol for 13 years and says his wife got him out of a police-only circle of friends and to think beyond patrol. They took turns locking one another in a room to study for the next exam. Both had become lieutenants.

The couples were unanimous that they had a special level of understanding regarding the job. They could communicate without always putting things in words. They understood both when a partner wanted to talk something out or not talk. They felt their marriages helped them to be less cynical about the job and see that they were able to help many people in spite of the tragedies.

They seemed flexible about dividing up household chores and put a premium on their time together, although, as individuals, each had a special interest outside work and home—rodeoing, writing science fiction, playing on a softball team, tournament bridge.

Sue Chance, who is a psychiatrist, was impressed by the women's sense of doing their jobs their own way, and the authority they exuded. She was also impressed by how proud their husbands were of them, proud that their wives had won medals or were better known for their accomplishments than they. Along the same line, husbands *knew* their wives were well-trained and capable of protecting themselves.

Handling Family Responsibilities

Back to Susan Martin's sample. Fourteen of the men and twelve of the women were parents. But while only one of the men was a single parent, ten of the 12 women were and all were 30 years old or younger (p. 59). Behind these figures is probably the biggest difference between these young Washington, DC officers—the extent to which marriage and family plans affected career plans. Martin said marriage and family had positive effects on the men's aspirations and performance. But they had just the opposite effect upon the women (pp. 73–74).

The effect upon their careers of the women hoping to get married and have families were these: compared to the men, more wanted inside assignments with regular hours that would mesh more easily with raising a family; their expectations of promotion in five years were less optimistic; they were less willing to predict what their work futures would be. While 10 women could make no prediction about the future, only 5 men were that uncertain. Martin said that none of the men expected family plans to adversely affect their careers, while the women, in contrast, were powerfully influenced by the conflicting demands on their time that working and having a family would involve (p. 72).

Martin noted that changing shifts every two weeks and frequent court appearances of uncertain length make being a mother very difficult. And since the expectations of women as parents are traditionally greater than those of men as parents, the role strains for women police are much greater (p. 74).

Another piece of evidence that families can be negative motivators for women is found in the details of Powers' (1983) study of the motivations of Sacramento women police cadets and officers. These women were chiefly motivated for police work by interesting assignments, helping others, and salary. "Influence of family members" was at the bottom of their motives lists. In explaining why family was a negative factor, Powers tells us that cadets and officers alike wrote comments to the effect that they were afraid of what the job did to family life. One woman had already had two divorces due to being a police officer, and another woman lamented that living the reality of changing shifts was totally different from anticipating it.

LIFESTYLES

This could be a fascinating section, but thus far lifestyles have only been the subject of newspaper and magazine articles.

For example, here are some of the details of the lifestyle of one 31-year-old county police sergeant who has a high school teacher husband and two small children. The byline for her Sunday newspaper profile read, " 'Sheriff Sue' Rahr makes kids her Number 1 priority, her own, or someone else's" (Young, 1988).

Rahr was the only girl in a family of six boys. Growing up she liked to push her baby brothers around the neighborhood in a stroller and help her mother cook and clean. In school she was involved in drama, cheerleading, and the drill team. She got "recruited" in college by taking a police science class and went on to get a bachelor's degree in police science. She says people describe her as "feminine-looking." When her first son was born, she tried opening a day-care center but it didn't pay the bills, so she has a nanny take care of her children. She has worked for nine years as a police officer—on patrol, in crime prevention, narcotics, and the warrants unit. Currently she heads a special assault unit that investigates child abuse and sex crimes against adults. She is praised for her organizing ability and her ability to repair relationships among alienated departments. She is described as a hard worker, someone good at encouraging people to do their best, someone with style, class, and dignity, who leaves victims feeling that the police really care about them.

She used to work out in a gym and run three miles a day but now her exercise and recreation appear to revolve around her little boys. She talks about her home and children as stress reducers. She keeps the two worlds of work and home separate but is equally committed to both. Her husband says that despite her emphasis on family, he can't see her ever leaving police work. It's easier for him to picture her at the top, as a police chief or sheriff.

To make a success of policing, as Sue Rahr has done, requires support from colleagues, friends, and close family members like Sue's very supportive husband. What is known about women officers' families' attitudes, in general?

Lovers' and Families' Attitudes

Janus, Janus, Lord, and Power's (1988) questionnaire, taken by 135 fulltime sworn women police from the New York City Department and environs, asked this mostly not married (72 percent) group how much support they got from their sexual partners. Fully 57 percent said their lovers' response was supportive, and only 23 percent said it was unfavorable (another 20 percent described the reaction as neutral). How did their sexual partners react to the authority of their being a police officer? Equivocally. Twenty-four percent of the officers said their partners' reaction was positive, 23 percent said negative, and the majority said neutral. The authors say women under age 28 got more support from lovers, and women over 35 significantly less support.

The women's families of origin had been largely neutral toward the idea of women in police work (50 percent), with 22 percent of families unfavorable and 28 percent favorable. However, once the women were on the job, only 12 percent of their families remained neutral. Now 70 percent had favorable attitudes and only 18 percent were unfavorable. Almost half of these women, interestingly, had relatives in law enforcement.

Janus et al. report that only 21 percent of the women said that schedules and tours of duty *did not interfere* with their social life. Thirty-eight percent said time schedules "much" and "very much" conflicted with their social life.

How important were men to these women's social lives? Men were "very important" to 39 percent and "important" to 46 percent. Fourteen percent said "so-so," and only 1 percent said men were unimportant. The importance of men can also be seen from the fact that 68 percent said they were more comfortable with men officers, while only 5 percent said they were more comfortable with women officers (and 27 percent said "both").

Fourteen of 25 women officers Wexler and Logan (1983) interviewed were single and dating men. Ten of them, 71 percent, were having trouble doing so because the men couldn't accept their occupation. They recall the fate of previous relationships held by the women who graduated from the New Jersey State Police' all-female class. By the end of the five months, as a consequence of their "new mental attitude," many had broken up with their boyfriends (Patterson, 1980).

Career Commitment

Weisheit (1987) studied 42 women and 191 men sworn officers of the Illinois State Police. These officers work in rural areas, doing mostly patrol work in single-officer vehicles. The women were significantly younger than the men, 27 years on the average compared to 39 years for the men. In fact, only 3 women were over 30. There was also a huge difference in the amount of police experience they had. The men averaged 13 years, the women 3 years.

The officers indicated the likelihood that they would stay in policing until retirement. Only 3 percent of the men but 19 percent of the women said they would "probably" or "certainly" leave policing before retirement. While this is a significant difference between the sexes, even when age was taken into account, 19 percent is hardly a severe indictment of women's career commitment.

In fact, Weisheit raised this issue. Is career commitment what was measured by this item or was it the conflict between commitments to policing and to the role of wife and mother? Seventy-nine percent of the women and 70 percent of the men agreed that women were more likely than men to have conflicts between the demands of jobs and families. Weisheit quotes the comment of a mother of two children under age four who had been a public servant for 14 years and with the state police 5 years. She felt she now had to devote her primary energy to her children and lamented that the state police would not let her take an extended leave until the children were school age. She was resigning and predicted the police would have problems with all women who had to decide somewhere along the line about what was Number One, the police service or their families.

Two other indirect measures from Weisheit's study of the women's career commitment were that 86 percent of them would encourage their daughters (as well as their sons) to enter policing, and 75 percent of their male colleagues said women had to work harder than men to get proper credit for their work.

BACKGROUND DIFFERENCES FROM MALE COLLEAGUES

An interesting aspect to looking at the demographics of women police is the extent to which they are like and unlike the men they work with. We would expect the typical department's women to be younger than the men because of women's recent entry into the field. We might also expect the women to have more education than the men, less experience in the service, and lesser rank as a function of less experience. Here are some examples from the research studies included in this book of the demographic differences which may exist across the U. S. in the women and men police officers who are working together.

In Fry and Greenfield's (1980) sample of patrol officers, the men were older and had less education. For example, 44 percent of the men were under 31 years old compared to 57 percent of the women. And 41 percent of the men had "some college" versus 62 percent of the women.

Vega and Silverman (1982) studied 826 people of whom as many as 53 were women. The median age of the men was 30, of the women 26. The median years of police service for the men was six years versus only 2 years for the women. Seventy-five percent of the men were married, 33 percent of the women. Sixty-six percent of the men had attended college versus 80 percent of the women. At least politically, they were alike: 60 percent of both groups were Democrats, 25 percent Republicans. And racially 96 percent of the men were white, as were 97 percent of the women.

Hunt, McCadden, and Mordaunt (1983) collected their data from six law enforcement agencies. They had a total of 1,101 men and 68 women (6 percent). Compared to the men these women were more often black, had less experience as police officers, and were less often in command positions. Half of the women had 3 or more years of college versus 35 percent of the men.

Homant and Kennedy (1985) studied 62 women and 89 men. The women were significantly younger, had less police job experience, less experience specifically dealing with family fights, and worked more in rural areas. However, the really big differences between the women and the men were in education and marital status. Seventy percent of the women had baccalaureate degrees versus 26 percent of the men. And only 43 percent of the women were married versus 82 percent of the men.

Wexler and Quinn (1985) studied 122 men and 21 women who were planning on taking an upcoming promotional exam for sergeant. Looking at years on patrol the women were at a decided disadvantage. Three years or less experience were reported by 14 percent of the men versus 45 percent of the women; 10 percent of the women had no patrol experience at all. Sixty-seven percent of the men had 6–10 years on patrol versus 15 percent of the women.

Meagher and Yentes (1986) surveyed 20 women and 34 men from a Midwestern state. The median age for the men was 35, for the women 32. Eighty-eight percent of the men were white, as were 80 percent of the women. The sexes did not differ in median education, 14 years. They differed greatly in police experience, the men having a median of 11 years, the women 4 years.

THE DOUBLE STANDARD

If there is an "issue" to this chapter, it is the question of women police being held to a stricter moral standard than men in their lifestyles.

Does a double standard of acceptable personal behavior exist? Are women judged more harshly? Are they under more scrutiny for instances of immoral conduct? Are men less likely than women to suffer disciplinary action for off-duty activities below "acceptable standards?"

A little article, "Out-of-wedlock pregnancy cannot serve as basis for termination," in the *Police Chief* (1986) points out a basic difference between the lifestyles of men and women officers: more women than men are single parents. But the point of bringing up this story here is to illustrate that as far as lifestyles go, some police agencies continue to use a double standard.

In this out-of-wedlock case, Officer Owens, a Jennings, La. officer was discharged for immoral conduct for being pregnant with her second out-of-wedlock child. Louisiana law gives the police the right to terminate employees for engaging in dishonest, disgraceful or immoral conduct. The courts found, however, that the regulation prohibiting immoral conduct did not define what it was or give standards for judging officers' behavior. Without standards the courts could not rule that an out-of-wedlock pregnancy was immoral conduct. Had Officer Owens been married, her pregnancy would not have been grounds for discharge. Had she had sexual relations and not become pregnant, she would not have been discharged. Male officers who had premarital or extramarital sexual relations were not disciplined under the regulation banning immoral conduct. So Officer Owens' termination, the court said, was sex discrimination: she had been terminated for acts male officers could commit with impunity. She was ordered reinstated with back pay.

Probably the most celebrated cases involving the double standard are those of Barbara Schantz and Cibella Borges who both posed nude for magazines (Lawson, 1983). Officer Schantz was suspended for 37 days for violating the Springfield, Ohio department's code of ethics by posing for the centerfold of *Playboy*. Women officers are quoted as not approving of her behavior and feeling that it reflected badly on women as a whole, *but* they also defended her First Amendment right to express herself as well as her right to make extra money so that she could buy a house for the son she was raising alone.

Officer Borges had posed *before* she joined the New York City police as a sworn officer. But the pictures weren't published until she was on the force and when they appeared she was suspended without pay and then fired for discrediting the department and behaving "well below" acceptable standards of personal and professional behavior. Once again women officers were said to feel the pictures were awful, but that Borges had had them taken before she became an officer. They felt it was not sufficient reason for her to lose her job given that men did worse things and didn't lose their jobs.

Schantz got her job back by apologizing to the public and saying she violated the rules . . . and also by agreeing to drop a $1,000,000 law suit she and *Playboy* filed against the police challenging her suspension.

SUMMARY

To sum up this chapter, background information on women police is extremely sketchy. Compared to men police, women police appear to be less married and more educated. They seem to come to the police service from low level Service and Organizational jobs. They have far greater conflicts between the demands of the job and family responsibilities than men do. And compared to the men, the emotional and social support they get from families and friends is problematic. The one fact we can be certain of is much, much more about their backgrounds remains to be researched. While job application forms in personnel files may not be the most abundant source of background data, surely more could be done with them than I was able to find.

Chapter 4

PERSONALITY TRAITS

The twenty-eight Washington, DC women officers Susan Martin (1980) studied were different from other women in that many described themselves as independent, athletic, or tomboys when they were growing up. Several had already thought about nontraditional careers in the military and police, so that when the opportunity suddenly arose, they took it (pp. 61–62).

Alice Fleming's (1975) book based on interviews with women in the New York Police Department supports Martin's picture of independence and assertiveness. Some of the words Fleming chose to describe NYPD women as they rescued would-be suicides and played the undercover role of "Muggable Mary," were courageous, scrappy, quick-thinking, persistent and indefatigable.

And although Mary Ellen Abrecht (1976) didn't use adjectives to describe her personality in *The Making of a Woman Cop*, to me she displayed enormous energy, driving around doing her sergeant's job while going to law school at night. She was also very brave even when scared, assertive in her dealings with overly watchful superiors, tough and feisty to citizens and male colleagues alike when they challenged her authority. But the main characteristic that made for her success was not a personality trait—it was her very high intelligence.

Observational accounts such as Martin's, Fleming's, and Abrecht's leave us with the impression that personality-wise, today's women police seem to be adventurous, outdoorsy, independent, and energetic. What have the "personality studies" discovered? How valid are these broadbrush descriptions? But first, some historical perspective.

HISTORICAL TRAITS OF WOMEN POLICE

Lois Higgins (1961, pp. 27–40) believed women police possessed instinctive maternal kindness and sympathy. As interrogators and interviewers they should have a wide range of interests, be observant and intellectually curious, and keenly interested in how the human mind works. Especially in interrogating children, a woman's maternal tendencies and inherent affection for children were to keep the atmosphere friendly. Women's naturally kind, sympathetic approach was only acquired by male officers after long study and experience. Higgins seemed to regard women's personalities as one of their strengths for specialist police duties, friendliness being their most indispensable trait.

Higgins also noted that women remained calm, composed, and unimpressed when women suspects tried to elicit sympathy by resorting to tears and self-pity. Men, on the other hand, became confused and lost control in such situations (p. 31).

Daniel Bell (1982) has given us a decade-by-decade rundown on the personality traits police departments have felt were important. In the 1930s, in addition to a good education and social work experience, women were supposed to have a pleasant personality, a positive attitude toward women with problems, tolerance, common sense, sympathy, and emotional stability. In the 1940s, in addition to being college graduates, women were not to be overly feminine and sentimental, but also not too aggressive, mannish, or callous. They were thought better adjusted if they had lots of extracurricular social activities and were neat and well-groomed.

By the 1950s women were required to be dignified, alert, sensible, tactful, and sympathetic. Their personal appearance was to be neat, attractive, and command respect, and the mark of a well-adjusted personality was being more interested in others than in oneself.

Such personal characteristics are consonent with the specialist role of women, that is, using women to investigate cases of juvenile delinquency and to patrol public places and recreational facilities to protect the morals of females and juveniles.

What are the personalities of women police like today? How do they compare with other women? How do they compare with men police? Two issues seemed to have dominated researchers' minds—to what degree might women sacrifice their "femininity," and to what degree must they adopt the "masculine police personality," to be accepted and satisfied with their jobs?

WOMEN AND THE
TRADITIONAL "POLICE PERSONALITY"

Berg and Budnick (1986, 1987) see a relationship between women officers' job satisfaction and adopting a masculine personality. Not a "mainstream" masculine personality, either. Rather a combination of authoritarianism, assertiveness, cynicism, aggressiveness, and a sense of isolation from ordinary folks, the traditional "police personality." Berg and Budnick maintain that to be successful in police work, women's personalities must be masculine to begin with, or become masculine, starting in the police academy. They cite studies which suggest that women must exhibit at least some masculine traits to be accepted by male peers.

Berg and Budnick associate masculine traits with satisfactorily performing general patrol duties, and, later, specialized unit duties such as homicide and crime scene investigations. They associate feminine traits with satisfactorily performing *only* subordinate, non-field jobs such as matron, meter maid, and victim's assistant. In their view, caretaking and nurturance have little to do with patrol or command positions.

Kennedy and Homant (1981) gathered some data to see if, compared to other women, women police had personalities that were more masculine, for example, more aggressive and authoritarian, than the average woman. If women police were less feminine than other women, they could conform closer to the masculine idea of an ideal patrol officer. On the other hand, being less feminine would also mean that the hoped-for benefits of a "policewoman's personality" would never come about. What benefits? Kennedy and Homant said women were theorized to precipitate less violence, reduce violence in men officers, improve community relations, deal better with other women, and get more citizen cooperation and assistance.

Kennedy and Homant compared 44 Detroit area women police with 62 registered nurses who were completing bachelor's degrees at the University of Detroit. The personality measure they used was short and global, good for differentiating groups, but not so good at providing detailed individual profiles. This short form of the California Psychological Inventory thus produced three scores on which to compare the two groups of women: Modernity, Femininity, and Socialization.

The women police were significantly both more modern and less feminine than the nurses. Which is probably a surprise to no one. The femininity items measured interests according to traditional masculine-feminine stereotypes, so finding the police less stereotypically "feminine" makes sense. The modernity items measured self-assurance and openness to new experiences. Again, finding the police more "modern," defined this way, is not unexpected. Women with this combination of scores, they say, would seldom be described as "shy," "silent," "cautious," "timid," or "mild."

Janus, Janus, Lord, and Power (1988) were concerned about how the job might have diminished women officers' feminine identification. They asked 135 officers in the New York City area, the majority between ages 28–35 and 44 percent with 3–10 years of service, if any aspect of the job had caused them to feel a loss of femininity. Thirty-eight percent said yes, but 62 percent said no. The women were also asked if they attributed successful outcomes of calls to being a woman. Sixty-two percent said "occasionally," and a third reported "often." Only 2 percent said "never" (and 13 percent didn't answer). On the other hand, 55 percent also said they had been assigned demeaning tasks solely because they were women.

Now for the trait of authoritarianism. Compared to men officers, women officers have been found to be significantly *more authoritarian,* at least in Texas and Oklahoma (Davis, 1984). Texas and Oklahoma women police saw the world more in terms of the weak versus the strong, and leaders as needing to be strict to gain respect. The women's greater authoritarianism was coupled with greater cynicism and being more hardnosed about overlooking infractions than men.

Women criminal justice students, on the other hand, have been found to be significantly *less authoritarian* than men students. Austin and O'Neill (1985) gave the 20-item Rokeach Dogmatism Scale to 102 men and 98 women with law enforcement or criminal justice college majors. Two-thirds of these women were juniors and seniors, and two-thirds of them attended a residential university in the Midwest, while the remainder attended a Midwest commuter college. Twenty-nine percent seemed destined for a career in law enforcement, while 32 percent were going into corrections and 30 percent into the courts.

Dogmatism or close-mindedness is generally considered equivalent to authoritarianism. A typical item might refer to freedom of speech as a worthy goal but to the necessity of restricting it in certain political groups. The extent to which a person agrees with an item such as this adds to her or his Dogmatism score.

Austin and O'Neill's concern was whether people in law enforcement came to it more authoritarian than other people, or whether they are socialized to become authoritarian on the job. They also addressed the issue of whether recruiting more women to law enforcement would change the traditional, male "police personality." Their answer is both no and yes. First, they dismiss the statistically significant difference between the men and women as having no practical importance inasmuch as sex as a variable accounted for a small proportion of the variation in authoritarianism scores. But they then go on to say that recruitment of women may decrease existing levels of authoritarianism in criminal justice occupations.

Clearly, if we want a definitive answer to the question of whether women and/or men are predisposed to authoritarianism before they become police officers, or are socialized by the police occupation to become authoritarian, or both, many more studies need to be added to those of Davis and Austin and O'Neill.

The evidence for changing the police organization via a different, "woman police" personality is equivocal. Being "less feminine" implies less change in the overall police personality. But being "more modern" implies great change insofar as men police are among the lowest scorers on modernity (Homant, 1983). Women being less authoritarian than men before entering the police service is hopeful, but becoming more authoritarian afterward certainly is not.

What society wants, although it may take decades, is what society will get. Do we want the occupation of police officer to be associated with what is stereotypically "masculine" work with overtones of competition, assertiveness, and technological know-how? Or do we want the occupation to become androgynous, an occupation that demands both stereotypically masculine and feminine personality traits in its practitioners?

A BROAD COMPARISON WITH WOMEN IN GENERAL

How much alike are women police officers' personalities and those of women in general? Lester, Gronau, and Wondrack (1982) compared 33 women state police recruits near the end of training with 31 women college students. The women did not differ in age (early twenties), height, weight, or years of college (2 plus).

Lester et al. compared the two groups first on Bem's androgyny scale which is an adjective checklist and generates three kinds of scores, femininity, masculinity, and androgyny.

The two groups were alike in their femininity scores but significantly different in their masculinity scores. As one might expect, the women police described themselves as more masculine (which also made their androgyny scores more masculine and significantly different from the control women). Lester et al. comment that the recruits appeared to have added masculine traits to their personalities without losing any of their feminine traits. For example, they said they were more assertive, forceful, risk-taking, athletic, self-sufficient, competitive, and more acting like a leader, at the same time that they described themselves as just as feminine as the college students.

Twenty-seven of the recruits' scores tended toward masculinity, and six toward femininity, as compared to the students, where half tended toward masculinity and half toward femininity.

Lester et al.'s recruits also took a tried-and-true personality inventory known as the Edwards Personal Preference Schedule. "The Edwards" measures fifteen personality needs. The idea here was to compare the women recruits with the norms for adult females and with the scores of 90 male recruits.

First, let me give a bit of elaboration as to what a person's need for "affiliation" or "order" or "intraception" means on "The Edwards." The fifteen scales measure the following needs:

1. Achievement: need to accomplish and be outstanding, to be recognized.
2. Deference: need to follow others, to conform, to do what's expected.
3. Order: need to have things neat, scheduled, planned and organized.
4. Exhibition: need to be noticed by others, be the center of attention.
5. Autonomy: need to be independent and self-directed.
6. Affiliation: need to have lots of friends and do things with friends.
7. Intraception: need to analyze others' feelings and behavior.
8. Succorance: need to be helped by others, have friends' support.
9. Dominance: need to direct others, be a leader, supervise.
10. Abasement: need to feel guilty, depressed, inferior, and timid.
11. Nurturance: need to help others, to treat others with kindness.
12. Change: need to try the new, different, experimental.
13. Endurance: need to persist, to complete any task, put in long hours.
14. Heterosexuality: need for active heterosexual behavior.
15. Aggression: need to speak aggressively, to blame others.

Now, compared to the norms for adult females, the recruits had *higher* scores on the needs for achievement, exhibition, intraception, dominance, change, and heterosexuality. They also had *lower* scores for deference, order, affiliation, succorance, abasement, and endurance. Lester et al. look at all this and declare that women police appear to be "quite psychologically healthy." Certainly the only higher score that is dubious in terms of mental health is the recruits' higher exhibition score. But if it reflects greater self-confidence than the average woman has, then it doesn't seem so inappropriate. Higher exhibitionism may also be related to being highly visible and continually watched by the men to see how well they performed.

As far as their lower scores are concerned, it is not mentally healthy, in the extreme, to follow and be guided by others (deference). Nor to want to be supported by others all the time (succorance). Nor to have the poor self-image that a high need for abasement implies. So these lower scores all support the notion of solid mental health. But what do we make of the recruits' lesser needs to be organized, to have lots of friends, and to complete any task begun? Perhaps at this point we need to remember that on "The Edwards," you can't get high scores on everything. When one score goes up, another has to go down, because the testtaker is always choosing between two options. The thing to remember is overall, this group of young women was in better shape psychologically than Edwards' norm group.

COMPARISONS WITH MEN POLICE

Ann McCarron (1985), based on her observations as director of public safety at a university, thinks women are "predestined" from the beginning in law enforcement to be different from men. They are expected to react differently on patrol, expected to supervise differently, and expected as administrators to run a different kind of shop.

She feels women's different patrol techniques and ways of doing the job are really a matter of personality style differences. The police service has always made allowances for style differences among men, and she asks that women be accorded the same courtesy. As a result of expectations that they will be weaker and more deferential, women police work harder, she says, feeling driven to prove themselves capable. One area where a woman's sex-role socialization comes in handy is picking up the information men exchange in the locker room. Women's better listening skills must compensate for what McCarron considers their "biggest disadvantage."

In spite of such traditional expectations of women's weakness, the recruits in Lester et al.'s (1982) study had some amazing differences in quite the opposite direction. Women recruits had lower needs for deference, order, abasement and endurance than the men, and higher needs for exhibition, autonomy, dominance, change, and heterosexuality. While Lester et al. end their article by noting the "good deal of similarity" in the personalities of these men and women, I think the fact that the women differed from the men on nine of the 15 scales indicated not only that there were impressive differences between the personalities of women and men, but they pointed to women being more assertive and autonomous than men. Clearly, personality deserves to be researched more thoroughly and sex differences over time tracked.

Probably the widest-used psychological test in policing is the Minnesota Multiphasic Personality Inventory, the MMPI. It has been used for screening out deviants from the police service for decades. The MMPI has 13 scores which are often referred to by a letter or number. They are: 1, hypochondriasis; 2, depression; 3, hysteria; 4, psychopathic deviate; 5, masculinity-femininity; 6, paranoia; 7, psychasthenia; 8, schizophrenia; 9, hypomania; 0, social introversion; L, lying; F, a score to check on validity; and K, a score that indicates faking.

Despite the forbidding scale names to the MMPI, Bruce Carpenter and Susan Raza (1987) talk quite straight-forwardly about the MMPI data they gathered on 257 police applicants from a Southwestern state, comparing them to new norm groups of women and men tested in 1984, and also comparing these 237 men and 20 women to one another.

As a combined group, these police applicants' profiles showed them to be cheerful, outgoing, and effective in living. Also they had a strong interest in people, together with an interest in practical matters. Compared to the normative populations of men and women, these police applicants were *more* psychologically healthy. For example, fewer of them had elevated MMPI scores which suggest emotional difficulties. Interestingly, the police were more *homogeneous* as a group than the normative population, because, say the authors, they share the personality characteristics which lead one to desire to be a police officer.

The twenty women police compared to the normative female sample had the same degree of bodily concern and general anxiety. But the women police were less depressed, more psychologically mature, more assertive, and more aware of the needs of others. They were also more comfortable with interpersonal relationships and more likely to present a good impression of themselves.

How did the women police differ from the men? The women had higher scores on three of the thirteen scales suggesting that they were more assertive, energetic, and nonconforming compared to women in general than were the male police compared to men in general. That the women were more nonconforming than the men, in the sense of not identifying with traditional sex roles, is consistent with the job they were applying for.

It would have been a pleasure to have reported here a spate of studies inspired by Barbara Price's (1974) "Study of Leadership Strength of Female Police Executives." But, alas, they do not exist, so the classic will be elaborated upon instead, even though from the 1970s instead of the 1980s.

Price gave the Dynamic Personality Inventory (DPI) to 227 men and 26 women police executives (sergeants and above) in three Northeastern urban police departments. How did women's leadership potential compare with men's in terms of the personality traits associated with leadership?

It is very important to note that the definition of leadership adopted here was not some hypothetical ideal type. Rather, it was based on the personality traits previously shown to be present in *men* who had advanced upward within the police structure.

The women and men were compared on 11 leadership scales. On five scales their scores did not differ significantly—orality (control over social skills), exhibitionism, drive for achievement, social activities (extroversion), and initiative. On the other six scales, the women's and men's scores differed significantly. The women's scores were in the direction of stronger leadership on five traits, the men higher on one.

Here are descriptions of those six personality traits. Women were higher on "Emotional Independence" which measures a person's need for freedom of movement and emotional independence. They were also higher on "Verbal Aggression" which measures both self-assertive behavior verbally and intellectually. The women's higher "Social Roles" scores indicated that they sought out social roles and felt socially adequate.

On the two scales, "Conservatism" and "Concern with Appearance," which showed the largest differences between the women and the men, the women were *less* conservative, which is associated with leadership, and *more* concerned with appearance which measures a positive self-image and self-confidence. The scale on which the men scored higher was "Persistence," or reacting with renewed effort in the face of difficulties or opposition.

Price went on to make four other comparisons that have ramifications for how police organizations are administered. She found the women were significantly different from their male colleagues on all four characteristics — submissiveness, sadism, insularity, and creativity. She was concerned in these analyses with dispelling myths about the police. For example, that the police are more sadistic than the general population. The myth turns out to be false. These women police executives, however, were not only less sadistic than men in the general population, but less sadistic than their male counterparts.

The women were also less submissive than the men (there goes another myth), less insular (less hostile toward people of different backgrounds), and more creative. The women she studied, she said, appeared "creatively involved with a zest for life."

Does Price's conclusion hold today? Do women police executives still outscore men executives on personality traits associated with leadership? Finally, why didn't Price's last sentence — "the results are intriguing enough to justify further research" — come true?

THE "WOMAN POLICE OFFICER PERSONALITY"

Is there such a thing as a typical personality for women police officers in the U. S.? If Bryna Taubman (1987) for her book could concoct four composite characters based on the personality traits and personal characteristics of the dozens of New York City women police she interviewed, perhaps they can be compacted even further.

The following grand composite "woman police officer personality" is based on Taubman's "Geri," "Mary Frances," "Sophia," and "Sally."

This officer is definitely committed to her career. She believes in trying her best. She's annoyed at the way the job interferes with her social and family life, but she loves the excitement and variety of patrol and detective work. She is courageous, even when she's scared. She's learned to use a gun, but is more effective simply threatening suspects that she will shoot if she has to. She thus uses "feminine wiles," when she has to, to get the job done.

She brings a different perspective to the job, sees things differently than the men do, hears things men ignore, picks up on more detail. She likes working with a partner and as a team. Rather than rely on physical strength, she uses common sense. She's levelheaded, calming, respectful and friendly with citizens. She is sympathetic and especially understanding of women's problems and handling teenagers and children. She is particularly concerned with crimes against women, crimes involving women—wife abuse, child molestation, rape, prostitute abuse. She likes interesting assignments and the challenge of police work, but not administration and power.

She's willing to talk about her feelings with other women and men who try to understand a woman's point of view. She's resiliant and thick-skinned about harassment, frustrated and cynical about the courts, but maintains her compassion in spite of seeing the worst in people and the worst that can happen to people. Her family, home chores, and pets take up her time when she isn't at work and she doesn't have much time for recreation. But she likes reading and movies, getting dressed up to go out to dinner, and now and then, drinking and dancing.

So now the question is, are women police across the country like the women of the NYPD? If there is a research area where we could probably find out what we want to know just by looking in the files, it is the area of personality traits. Why? Because departments do psychological screening, and this means thousands of personality inventories have been administered over the past decade.

Personality tests have other purposes than spotting deviants; they could inform, describe, flesh out the portraits of women police who are hired, who stay, who get promoted, who are leaders. They can document personality differences from men police; they can chart change in the personalities of recruits from one decade to another. They can even answer that all important question—is the police organization changing women's personalities or is the "woman police officer personality" changing the organization?

Chapter 5

VALUES, ATTITUDES, AND INTERESTS

Among the attitudes, values, and interests observed by Sandra Jones (1986) among 110 British women police were a service-orientation toward the job, greater commitment to home than career, and a positive attitude toward emotionality in the workplace. These are broad, general, vocational interests and attitudes, the sorts of topics in which I expected to find American researchers interested as well.

But that is not the case, thus far. There has been only one major study of occupational interests in women police, and researchers curious about their values and attitudes have focused on very specialized topics—how women police feel about domestic violence, child abuse, cynicism, egalitarianism, and male-female roles.

We will take up values and attitudes first and then look at the interests of women officers as measured by a traditional career counseling test, as well as by the activities toward which women gravitate after they enter policing.

WOMEN'S VALUES AND DOMESTIC VIOLENCE

Domestic violence is thought by many people to be linked with female officers' values because as women they are expected to be more sensitive to women's issues such as spouse abuse.

Because battered women have perceived the police in general as more helpful after a woman officer had responded to their calls, Homant and Kennedy (1985) set out to see if women and men officers had different attitudes toward family fights.

They compared 62 women police, most of them members of Women Police of Michigan, with 89 men police in nonsupervisory positions. They collected a host of background data—marital status, age, education, length of service, etc.—to correlate with scores on a nine-item "Involvement in Family Fights" scale.

A high Involvement score meant showing professional concern and deriving personal satisfaction out of handling family fights in a helpful and effective way. The items that went into the scale came directly from what the battered women had told the authors. These women wanted to be shown understanding and concern, but, at the same time, they wanted officers to remain fair and impartial. *And* the women wanted to be given information about their rights, options, and shelter homes. The antithesis of Involvement is a passive, cynical attitude that makes one leave the situation as soon as possible, and *not get involved.*

Homant and Kennedy found sex strongly correlated with scores on the Involvement Scale. The women officers' mean score was significantly higher than the men's mean score. The items on which the sexes differed the most had to do with making sure that women knew about shelter homes and getting them there, and showing sympathy and understanding. At the same time there were also big differences in the attitudes of the women and men toward accepting family violence as normal, even marital rape as normal, men being more accepting.

Only one other background variable besides sex of officer was related to Involvement in Family Fights—level of education. The greater the officers' education, men or women, the more *involved* they were.

Homant and Kennedy speculated that Involvement is related to two other attitudes: Feminism and Concern for Women's Victimization.

They measured Feminism and Concern for Women's Victimization each with one item. Feminism was measured by agreement/disagreement with a statement having to do with the women's movement being a good thing for society. Concern was measured by the question of which family member was more likely to get injured in a fight, the man or the woman.

These authors' speculations were confirmed. The women's mean Feminism score was higher than the men's, and on the Concern item the women felt significantly more strongly that it would be the woman in the dispute who would get injured. Men officers were also less sympathetic toward women on two other items, where the men believed more than women officers that women in family fights are basically at fault. *And* that women are the more difficult sex for the police to deal with.

Homant and Kennedy's motivation for this study was to propose a better way for the police to respond to family violence. Judging from the reactions of the shelter women, one solution would be simply to put women police on every domestic trouble call. But this would be inequitable to women officers who, no matter how important they feel such runs are, may feel penalized for taking an extra share of domestic trouble. The authors' recommendation for departments was to institute discussion groups in which women and men could discuss their different points of view about family violence and different styles of dealing with it.

Michael Breci (1987) also looked into background factors and attitudes of police officers towards intervening in family fights. And out of the same motivation as Homant and Kennedy, that is, to provide administrators with information about how different officers might respond to new programs and policies concerning family violence.

Do women and men officers have different attitudes toward intervening in family fights? This was the question Breci asked of 242 officers responsible for handling domestic disputes. They were 220 men and 22 women officers from four law enforcement agencies, two in the Midwest, two in the Southeast. The smallest agency employed 48 officers, the largest 215 officers. The percent of blacks in the populations of these cities varied greatly from 0.3 percent to 40 percent.

In contrast to Homant and Kennedy's findings, Breci found no difference between male and female officers in attitudes toward family fights. Men and women agreed to the same extent that intervening *is real police work,* and that while the public saw them as authority figures, they saw themselves as service providers.

Similarly, both women and men thought that tough arrest laws would not deter domestic violence, and that instead, officers should be trained to help couples resolve their differences.

The one variable which gave Breci a guideline as to how a police department might implement training for family violence was educational background. Better educated officers were more in favor of formal training programs than less well educated officers. The less well educated preferred to be taught on the job by more experienced officers. Interestingly, given the importance of education in determining attitudes here, only 48 percent of the women in Breci's sample had completed college, whereas 70 percent of the women in the Homant and Kennedy study were college graduates.

Going back to Homant and Kennedy's (1985) finding that men officers were more accepting of marital rape, it puzzles me that I could not find a study which examined possible differences in women and men police' attitudes toward rape. The closest thing to such a study was research done by Lester, Gronau, and Wondrack (1982). They did not address the issues of sex differences in attitudes toward rape, but they did find that women police recruits and women college students differed very little in their attitudes toward rape. They agreed to the same extent that sex was a motivation for rape, power was a motivation for rape, and victims did not precipitate rape (although the recruits thought women played a slightly greater role). They also had the same (unfavorable) perception of women after rape, the same perception that rape should be severely punished, and, as to how much resistance women should offer, the recruits indicated slightly more resistance than the students.

WOMEN'S VALUES VIS-A-VIS CHILD ABUSE

Another crime in which women police, stereotypically, are expected to differ in attitudes from men police is child abuse.

There is evidence from a college population that commonly feeds graduates into the police service—criminology students—that women feel child abuse and neglect are more serious acts than men do. Doerner (1987) had 221 students (and he does not tell us how many were male and female) in introductory criminology at a large southeastern public university rate 83 child abuse and neglect items on a nine-point scale ranging from "not very serious" to "very serious." There were fourteen types of items and for four of the types, the women rated abuse more seriously than the men: sexual abuse, parental use of alcohol and drugs, parental sexual mores, and parental supervision.

The most serious sexual abuse item referred to parents having sexual intercourse with their children. The most serious alcohol and drug item referred to both parents being drug addicts. An item having to do with parents permitting prostitution in the home was the most serious "sexual mores" item, and an item about drunken parents driving a car with their child inside was the most seriously rated "supervision" item. In contrast to these four types of items, the women did not differ from the men in ratings of, for example, medical abuse, physical abuse, or educational abuse. Thus, both sexes rated with the same degree of seriousness, items which referred to ignoring a child who was ill and not eating, burning a child with a cigarette, and not enrolling a child in school.

THE PROBLEM OF CYNICISM

Cynicism is an attitude historically and traditionally associated with policing. It is an important attitude because a cynical cop is the farthest thing from an ideal officer. Cynicism, if widespread, hurts not only individual police officers, but is very bad for police organizations. A cynical attitude makes it very difficult for the police to act like public servants and professionals and to identify with the goals and values of the criminal justice system.

What is the nature of cynicism among police officers? It is basically a distrustful attitude, a disbelieving, contemptuous attitude toward other human beings. It means a loss of faith in people and ideals. The police can be cynical about the public, the criminal justice system, the police organization, or all of the above.

One of my personal predictions about women police and cynicism was that women would *not* be as cynical as men. I believed that women would continue to be more optimistic and trusting of citizens, the police organization, and even of the system. Women more than men, my reasoning went, believe that they can be of service and make a difference in people's lives. Women can also hold on to their ideals longer than the men because as *outsiders* in the police service, they probably aren't exposed to as much fraternal grousing and complaining. Last, by virtue of being new to the system, women are open to change and better ways of doing the job. All of which is counter to cynicism.

Thus, imagine my surprise when I found the cynicism studies and, lo and behold, women officers are more cynical than men officers.

Dorsey and Giacopassi (1987) were interested in how eight variables affected cynicism, four demographic variables—age, race, sex, and education—and four work-related variables—shift, rank, precinct, and length of service. Seventy-nine men (58 whites, 21 blacks) and 89 women (44 whites, 45 blacks) with the Memphis Police Department completed their questionnaire which included the 20-item Neiderhoffer Cynicism Scale.

Four of the eight variables were significantly related to cynicism. *Rank* was important. Superior officers were much less cynical than patrol officers. *Tenure* was also important. The officers with the least (1–3 years) and the greatest (16–18 years) service were less cynical than the people with inbetween amounts. Rookies and officers looking toward retirement were the most optimistic. And *shift* was important. Officers who worked day shift were less cynical than officers who had to work other shifts.

The fourth background variable related to cynicism was sex. *Women were more cynical than men.* Cynicism scores could range from 20 to 100. The average scores for the 133 patrol officers in the sample were: white males, 61; black males, 54; white females, 63; black females, 60. And even though the numbers were very small for the four groups of *superior officers*, their mean cynicism scores were: white males, 49; black males, 50; white females, 58; black females, 54. Note that race was not related to cynicism, the average white score being 59, the average black score 58.

Is women's cynicism across the board, that is, are women officers equally disillusioned with the public, the courts, and the police organization itself? My prediction was that women would be primarily disillusioned with the police system itself. Disillusioned at the small numbers of women in the upper ranks. Disillusioned about their continued marginal status and the lack of respect and acceptance shown them by the men. My prediction was that they were probably more optimistic about the criminal justice system and about people in general than men, but that their cynicism about the police organization made them appear more cynical overall.

To prove me wrong we have only to look at Davis' (1984) findings and Remmington's (1983) findings. Davis first. He studied only one kind of cynicism, cynicism toward the public. He did it with just one questionnaire item involving agreeing or disagreeing with the notion that people obey the law out of fear of being caught. He found the same thing Dorsey and Giacopassi did. Among these officers from the states of Texas and Oklahoma, the 145 women were significantly more cynical than the 2,148 men officers.

This female cynicism about human nature did not change when minority women were excluded. Nor did controlling for age, rank, or socioeconomic status make any difference. One thing that did make a difference was education, but again, counter what I would have expected. *Women with more education were more cynical!* Davis speculated that better educated women had higher expectations for themselves in the police system which made sex discrimination even more disillusioning.

Remmington (1983), who rode along with the Atlanta Police and interviewed 50 officers during 1975–76 observed the same thing Davis found with his survey. Sadly, Atlanta women police, who were grossly discriminated against on a day-to-day basis by the men (through overprotection, domination, and verbal abuse) had become increasingly cynical and mistrustful in several ways.

The Atlanta women said policing had made them more conservative and negative toward the judicial system, the public, and friends and family. They showed their cynicism not by expressing frustration or resentment at male officers, but by doubting their own capabilities and by displaying a gruff, abrupt, and unsympathetic attitude toward the public, mimicking their male colleagues.

Davis, Remmington, and Dorsey and Giacopassi all point to sex discrimination as the reason for women officers' greater cynicism. Dorsey and Giacopassi speculate that the significant correlates of cynicism that they found among the Memphis police were related to job satisfaction. Officers who have been promoted may be more satisfied with their jobs than subordinate officers. Swing and night shift work is more stressful than the day shift, so people who have to work the less "normal" shifts are not as satisfied as those who work during the day. And while it is unacceptable to single out blacks and make fun of them, it is permissible to make fun of women officers. Thus, they suspect, the women may not only have been unsteeled to hostility from the public, but were not prepared for the lack of respect they experienced from male officers. The men's lack of acceptance made the women's jobs less satisfying and at the same time made the women more cynical.

ATTITUDES ABOUT EGALITARIANISM AND MALE-FEMALE ROLES

In 1979 Darrell Steffensmeier did a study with 89 women and 100 men who were studying criminology at a large eastern university. The majority of them were majoring in law enforcement and many aspired to become police officers. Steffensmeier was interested in the relationship between egalitarianism toward women police and having a traditional or contemporary outlook on sex roles.

Should there be just as many women as men police, should women have an equal chance to be chief, should police work be done primarily by men—these were the kinds of attitudes in his egalitarianism scale. Steffensmeier's results for the men students were quite dismaying. Seventy-nine percent of them thought men were better able to work with adult offenders and only 34 percent thought women were as able to do police work as men. What was primarily responsible for the men's attitudes, however, was their traditional sex role orientation. The women had both more egalitarian attitudes and a more contemporary attitude toward sex roles. Steffensmeier concluded that existing sex role attitudes were a severe obstacle for women seeking careers in law enforcement.

There have been three more recent studies dealing with egalitarianism which, fortunately, had more hopeful findings.

Women Cops Versus Nurses

Kennedy and Homant (1981) asked 44 women police and 62 nurses thirteen opinion questions of the strongly-agree to strongly-disagree variety that had to do with the role of the women police, the criminal justice system, and male-female roles. One of the things Kennedy and Homant thought most interesting about their data was that the women police and nurses differed so much on the item "I (would) like the job of a policewoman." They took it as evidence for how basically different the two groups of women were, despite the fact that the two groups only differed on two other opinion items.

The women police were more in favor of the police having more power and more against a woman police officer's role being limited to juvenile delinquency, sex crimes, traffic control and the like. Nothing remarkable there. But while both nurses and police described their jobs in favorable terms, only among the police were these correlations observed: Job satisfaction was highly correlated with *agreeing* that society is male-oriented and that women must stand up for their rights, and with *disagreeing* that women are not as good leaders as men. Thus, the more job-satisfied women police were, the more aware they were of male social dominance and rejected it.

The Ladycops Scale

Weisheit (1987) constructed a 14-item Ladycops scale which measures an egalitarian attitude toward women in policing with four kinds of items. Some items concerned the *public response,* for example, how citizens' confidence in the police might be affected by highly visible women in uniform. Other items had to do with preferential treatment to women by the *organization,* for example, items about women having an easier time at the academy or getting special assignments just because they were women.

A third type of item in the Ladycops scale had to do with the *women's performance,* for example, whether or not women who patrol alone are in greater physical danger than men. And last, there were items having to do with *male resistance,* such as an item which suggested that men do not like to be supervised by women. Not surprisingly, women officers scored higher on the Ladycops egalitarian scale than men officers, even when age was controlled for.

The Tampa Police

Vega and Silverman's (1982) sample of 826 police officers from the South responded to five general equality items. Here the amount of agreement displayed by the sexes was remarkable. Percentages agreeing, women first, followed by men, were as follows: women's place is at home, 25 percent, 50 percent; women are not discriminated against in the labor force, 50 percent, 50 percent; the first goal of women is raising a family, 25 percent, 50 percent; women should get equal pay for equal work, 90 percent, 90 percent. Both groups were also said to strongly favor women sharing equally in family decisions.

Regarding how people come to be more egalitarian, Vega and Silverman say a college education made these Tampa men more so. College men were more in favor of women on patrol and more positive toward riding with a new female officer than were noncollege men.

INTERESTS AS MEASURED BY THE KOIS

Before taking up "the Kuder," here is what the Strong-Campbell Interest Inventory (SCII), the most widely administered interest test, tells us about the vocational interests of women police. The following material is all taken from the SCII manual written by Hansen and Campbell (1985).

On the SCII the interests of women police are coded with one letter, "R," standing for "Realistic." Occupations can be coded with one letter, two letters, or three letters. The first letter designates the interest area which dominates the occupation, and any letters which follow mean that the people in that occupation have other strong, contributing interests, not as important as the first. The SCII divides up all occupations into six groups, RIASEC. There is the "R," or Realistic group. Then, "I" stands for Investigative, "A" for Artistic, "S" for Social, "E" for Enterprising, and "C" for Conventional.

For example, women Highway Patrol Officers' interests are coded "RCE" or Realistic, Conventional, and Enterprising, and men Highway Patrol Officers' interests are coded "RSE," Realistic, Social, and Enterprising. In both cases, realistic interests are primary, enterprising interests are tertiary. Highway patrol officers of both sexes have very similar profiles.

Another relevant example: women Secret Service Agents' interests receive a code of "ER" and men Secret Service Agents' interests a code of "RE." In this case, the women have stronger enterprising interests than the men, the men have stronger realistic interests than the women, but again, these are very similar profiles, which is what one would expect in an occupation.

What are the implications of women police having "Realistic" interests? First, they are very similar to men police officers in interests because the men, too, received a simple "R" code to their profiles.

Second, there are seven other "R" occupations for which the men and women have interest profiles that are coded simply as "R." These occupations are Air Force Officer, Bus Driver, Charter Bus Driver, Corrections Officer, Horticultural Worker, Metro Bus Driver, and Painter (meaning the house painting kind). What do all these people have in common, why are they "realistic"?

Having "Realistic" interests means having outdoor, technical, and mechanical vocational interests. The SCII manual says that people who score high on the "R" theme are practical and have good physical skills. They like to work outdoors and prefer working with things rather than ideas or people. They are supposed to have difficulty expressing themselves and communicating their feelings. Realistic people prefer occupations such as construction work, military jobs, the skilled trades (p. 14).

Some of this description seems to work for police officers, but some of it doesn't. The manual also tells us that police officers score high on three of the SCII's "Basic Interest" scales—Adventure, Military Activities, and Athletics. Police officers also score low on Art. So some facets to occupational interests police officers share with bus drivers and horticultural workers, while other facets they may not.

The samples of police officers (207 women, 294 men tested in 1979) on whom this SCII information is based were similar in age (women average age 32, men 33), in education (both had 15 years), but the men had 9 years experience to the women's six. Eighty percent of each group were assigned to patrol, investigative work, or a combination of the two. Clerical work took up 39 percent of the women's working hours, and it took up 42 percent of the men's time as well.

How do these SCII results compare with a second interest inventory, the KOIS?

Donald Zytowski and Kathleen Isgro recently administered the Kuder Occupational Interest Survey or KOIS to a random sample of members of the IAWP and reported their results in *WomenPolice* (1988). They say in this article that their findings were quite different from what male police officers had suggested female officers' interests were like. The men believed female officers' greatest interests were in social service and clerical activities.

Instead, the women showed their strongest interests to be in outdoor and mechanical activities. Outdoor interest is typically high in foresters, farmers, and naturalists. Mechanical interest is usually high in people who enjoy working with machines and tools such as car mechanics and aviators.

This IAWP sample showed the least interest in activities that were persuasive or computational. They weren't interested in the jobs of salespersons or buyers. And they were also not interested in working with numbers and solving mathematical problems.

The KOIS and SCII had complementary, mutually validating results. Women police, like men police, are basically "Realistic" in their vocational interests.

What was this group of women like? Their average age was 35 and average length of service 9 years. Over half (54 percent) would, upon starting over, choose law enforcement again. Only 12 percent said they would not. The remaining 34 percent would choose to be a police officer again if certain things were different. Chief among what they would like to see change was more opportunity for advancement and better pay. Zytowski and Isgro say the level of job satisfaction the women displayed was comparable to other professions such as lawyers and accountants.

Zytowski (1989) graciously made available the details of his study for this book and his various findings are reported throughout. Here we want to take a closer look at the interests of these 348 women.

In addition to showing testtakers how close their scores are to people in different occupations, such as police officer, the KOIS also produces ten broad, basic interest scores: Artistic, Clerical, Computational, Literary, Mechanical, Musical, Outdoor, Persuasive, Scientific, and Social Service.

Each woman officer thus had a top-ranked basic area of interest, a second-ranked area, etc. down to her tenth-ranked area. When these ranks are tallied for each of the ten areas for the whole group, median rank scores can be calculated. These overall rankings in turn give us an interest profile for women police.

Here, then, are the ten areas with their median ranks, arranged from highest to lowest: Mechanical, 3.08; Outdoor, 3.56; Scientific, 5.06; Musical, 5.13; Literary, 5.66; Clerical, 6.40; Social Service, 6.78; Persuasive, 7.16; Artistic, 7.44; and Computational, 7.64.

Males in general tend to score higher on the mechanical, computational, scientific, and persuasive scales, and females to score higher on the artistic, literary, musical, social service, and clerical scales (Aiken, 1985, p. 279). Thus, women police officers are like the average male in that they are most interested in mechanical (and outdoor) activities. They are not like the average male in that they are *not* interested in computational and persuasive activities.

Looking then at the areas where women typically score higher, women police are not typical women, particularly in their lesser interest in clerical, social service, and artistic activities.

INTERESTS AS PREFERRED ACTIVITIES WITHIN POLICING

Women are getting more and more interested in careers in criminal justice. The enrollment statistics of the School of Criminal Justice at Michigan State University showed that in 1970, 5 percent of 300 undergraduate majors were women. In 1984, 41 percent of 450 undergraduates were women! Sixty percent of these women were going to go into general duty police work. The rest wanted positions in juvenile justice, adult corrections, security, and criminalistics. And jobs were waiting for them, especially in large police departments with affirmative action programs (Radelet, 1986, p. 287).

Regarding this sixty percent of women criminal justice graduates who want to be police officers, the issue for some administrators and researchers still is, are women as a group more interested in certain police activities than others? Do women, on average, prefer clerical duties, handling juvenile and women victims and offenders, and other stereotyped female tasks? Or are their preferences for different police duties the same as the men's? What's the evidence?

Garrison, Grant, and McCormick (1988) asked a national sample of IAWP members what job assignments they preferred. By far the greatest number (44 percent) preferred uniform patrol. The next most popular assignments were crimes against persons (18 percent), administrative services (13 percent), and general detective work (11 percent). Only 6 percent preferred vice and 5 percent juvenile. This study offers virtually no support for the notion that women police today prefer to do traditional clerical and social service tasks. It may be that many women working in these traditional areas are not themselves responsible for these assignments.

On this same issue, Kathryn Golden (1982a, 1982b) got somewhat contradictory results working with two samples of law enforcement majors at a midwestern university. In the first study (1982a) she asked 126 men and 46 women students to divide up 100 percent among five activities police officers engage in, according to how they personally would like to spend their time. Here are the averages for how the women would like to spend their time: criminal investigation and arrest, 44 percent; helping citizens with other problems, 27 percent; resolving family disputes, 15 percent; writing reports, 11 percent; and "other," 4 percent.

The most important aspect to these percentages is that they did *not* differ from the men's percentages. These women going into law enforcement had exactly the same preferences and priorities for activities the men did. The women wanted overwhelmingly, as did the men, to solve crimes and avoid writing reports. They did, incidentally, correctly perceive on another survey item that about 17 percent of an officer's time is actually spent in criminal investigations and that much more time is devoted to helping citizens with other problems and administrative responsibilities, such as writing reports.

In her second study (1982b) Golden had 154 women and 134 men students rate nine criminal justice jobs on a scale of 0 to 4 in terms of how interesting they were. The women's interest in four traditional women's positions was significantly higher than the men's interest in them, the four jobs being probation officer with juvenile males, probation officer with juvenile females, youth service worker, and juvenile officer. Similarly, the women's interest in five traditional men's positions was significantly lower than the men's interest, the five jobs being patrol officer-rural, patrol officer-suburban, patrol officer-large city, detective-local police, and federal investigator.

So if we look at the preferred work activities of women and men going into law enforcement, we find no differences. But if we look at the job titles they prefer, sex differences appear. What does Golden say about the women's apparent attraction to these female-role-compatible specialties?

Golden notes that the two jobs that were of greatest interest to both women and men were detective and federal investigator. More than wanting to be in a low-paid, entry-level, traditionally female job, the women wanted a traditionally male job that had high prestige, a high salary, and which represented a promotion from the ranks. The women weren't so different from the men after all. What the women seemed to be saying was that if they had to work at a low level, they'd prefer female specialties to being on patrol.

Evidence that women *are* responsible for their gravitation toward traditional women's work within the police comes from Susan Martin's (1980) Washington, DC study. She noted the strong pull of "inside" assignments for women. More than men, the women wanted youth work, community relations jobs, and administrative positions (pp. 70–71).

Martin's observations help explain some findings, seldom discussed, in Bloch and Anderson's final report on the introduction of women into the Washington, DC police service, that is, the findings having to do with *assignment.*

Bloch and Anderson (1974) concluded that the new women were assigned to patrol less frequently than the new men. At the beginning of the research project, October 1972, the only difference was that the new women were assigned to station duty 11 percent of the time, twice as often as new men were. However, by August 1973, when supervisors no longer had to treat women equally, only 45 percent of the new women were on patrol compared to 71 percent of the men. Thirty-one percent of the women were now "inside," in clerical, the youth division, and community relations, compared to only 12 percent of the men. Twelve percent of the women also had "other street" assignments, such as the scooter squad, while only 4 percent of the men had "other street" duties.

Bloch and Anderson said the reasons for this difference in treatment were not clear. They noted that the women on the inside had more children than women with street assignments (65 percent compared to 47 percent). Interviews indicated that these inside jobs were willingly accepted. Bloch and Anderson wouldn't say whether the high frequency of station assignments was due primarily to the desires of the women or the attitudes of their supervisors. Martin, on the other hand, looking at the same department, felt it had more to do with the women's desires.

Martin's observations point to women gravitating toward inside clerical and social service activities because these activities were more interesting to them and because the work hours allowed them more easily to take care of family responsibilities. It is unfortunate that the most nontraditional tasks in policing continue to be associated with duty hours incompatible with raising children. A lot of what looks like choosing "female role-appropriate interests" and reducing "feelings of deviance for choosing a male career" may be nothing more than trying to find hours that allow one to take care of one's children.

Least Preferred Activities within Policing

Do women have a least preferred activity associated with policing? Every officer has her own particular aversion, but many women probably share the feelings of these New Jersey trainees about beating up other people.

The two biggest complaints of the women who dropped out of an all-woman trooper class run by the New Jersey State Police were the quasi-military atmosphere and boxing (Patterson, 1980). Both of these complaints are associated with the police as people who deliver force, including deadly force. The quasi-military atmosphere the women experienced was intense, as this particular state police organization had West Point type traditions such as wearing long-sleeved woolen shirts in the summer. Nine weeks of boxing training was apparently not liked by any of the women and during exit interviews, dropouts frequently cited boxing as the one aspect of training they found too hateful to endure.

The women who were able to finish the course, or "suffer through the demeaning military discipline" as one graduate put it, took on a whole new mental attitude. They had internalized the discipline and the necessity to push themselves beyond their previous limits and consequently now had a great deal of self-confidence and self-discipline. They now identified with the quasi-military environment and using their fists to hit other people. These former secretaries and doctor's assistants had become a part of the police elite.

SUMMARY

In line with stereotypical expectations about women's values, women police have been found to be more professionally involved in cases of domestic violence. They may also take sexual child abuse more seriously. Women police appear to be more cynical than men police. In researchers' minds, this greater cynicism is because of the sex discrimination women experience. Not surprisingly, women police are also more egalitarian and feminist in their attitudes than men police.

Regarding vocational interests, women police are not attracted to clerical and social service activities as the men might predict. But like men police they are most interested in practical, mechanical, and outdoor activities. Within policing, then, women's gravitation away from patrol to inside assignments is linked primarily with the desire for hours compatible with meeting family responsibilities.

Chapter 6

JOB MOTIVATION, JOB SATISFACTION

Women used to go into policing to help other people, men for the job security. Their roles in the police were so different, how could their motives have been the same? Small wonder, too, that many women came to the police from professions such as social work, nursing, and teaching, while many men had been semi-skilled workers, sales persons, and blue-collar tradesmen (Bell, 1982).

But how about today? Are the motivations of women and men becoming indistinguishable? Are men now equally interested in community service, and women as concerned as men about salary and security?

One might expect the motive "service to others" to be high in both men and women who have realistic, accurate perceptions of the job. For in reality, 80 to 90 percent of police activities are service in nature. Even patrol work, so long denied women, is basically service. However, even though policing is strongly social service, it is still strongly stereotypically masculine. How does that affect the motivations of women and men attracted to it?

And once on the job, how satisfied are women and men officers? Why do they stay? In addition to reviewing what is known about why women are attracted to the job, we will also take a look at why they get disillusioned and leave.

WOMEN OFFICERS' JOB MOTIVATIONS

Our search into motives and satisfactions will not be straightforward. The results, also, will be a little frustrating. This is because how questions are asked determines the answers they provide. When open-ended questions have been summarized by researchers, we simply have to trust those experts' judgments as to how participants responded. When questions are objective, we are limited by the alternatives offered by an investigator. After the fact, it's too late to say, why didn't you ask about "helping others" or the "importance of benefits?"

77

Here are three examples of what I mean by data ranging from expert opinion based on years of observation, to expert opinion based on interviews, to an objective questionnaire item that gave participants just four choices.

Clarice Feinman (1986), a criminal justice scientist at Trenton State College, describes women officers today as the "new professionals," maintaining that they closely resemble men officers in career goals. She says the current motivation of women for policing is salary, benefits, security, advancement, and the challenge of the job (p. 99). The opportunity to advance, says Feinman, is probably the greatest attraction for women college graduates, particularly minority women. And few jobs in the private sector offer the salary and benefits to women with high school diplomas and no special job skills.

Based on hundreds of interviews with women police over several years, Carol Ann Martin (1983) feels that they choose law enforcement because it is a field of opportunity for women and because they, as individuals, have had a lifelong ambition to be police officers. Of the women she has studied, less than one percent saw the police as a temporary career. To most it was a lifetime career and their chief reason for entering it was to help others.

And the final illustration of data on women's motives and satisfactions, the item, "Why did you choose police work as your profession?" Janus, Janus, Lord, and Power (1988) asked it of 135 New York City area women police ranging in age from 21 to 52. The two big reasons they gave were "self-gratification" (41 percent) and "financial reasons" (43 percent). Far less important were "idealism" (8 percent) and "prestige" (2 percent). These were the four alternatives presented and 6 percent of the women "didn't know" or wouldn't choose. "Financial reasons" is easy to understand, but "self-gratification" is the sort of answer that begs for clarification.

A Typical Local Study

A typical local study of women's job motives was done by Matthew Powers (1983) for the Sacramento Police Department. His goal was to design a more successful recruitment campaign for women. He noted that four motivational factors had seemed especially important in previous research—salary, benefits, helping others, and interesting work. Earlier studies of New York City women police, for example, found them to be most attracted by salary, followed by helping others, interesting work, and having a law enforcement orientation. But because different cities and regions of the country have different salary levels and employment policies, he felt that the safest strategy was for Sacramento to find out how women in their own locality rated various motives.

Powers got opinions not only from eight women cadets and seven officers; he also interviewed sixteen employment specialists—personnel directors, affirmative action officers and the like. The cadets and officers filled out a brief questionnaire; the specialists gave their comments over the telephone.

For the cadets the five top reasons in descending order were "interesting assignments," "adequate salary," "an opportunity to help others," "civil service benefits," and "advancement and promotion opportunities." There were eleven reasons in all and the least influential were "influence of family members," "desire to enter a male-dominated career field," and "influence of friends."

For the police officers the five top reasons in descending order were "interesting assignments," "an opportunity to help others," "advancement and promotion opportunities," "lifetime interest in law enforcement career," and "significant decision-making powers." Salary and benefits were ranked sixth and seventh. As with the cadets, the influence of friends and family and wanting to enter a male-dominated field were discounted.

The sixteen employment specialists supported what the women police said. They felt that women enter nontraditional work primarily for the salary, interesting work, and educational and training opportunities.

Powers said the fact that salary and interesting assignments came up consistently at the top of the three lists made them the two motivators to stress in Sacramento's recruiting materials, and that was just what they did.

Comparing Women's and Men's Job Motivation

There was amazing agreement between 20 women and 34 men officers from the Midwest in their personal reasons for choosing policing in a study reported by Meagher and Yentes (1986). At the top of both their lists were "opportunity to help people" and "security of the job." The next two reasons were also the same for both sexes—"excitement of the job" and "chance to fight crime." The two groups also agreed on reasons number five and six—"prestige of the occupation" and "a lifetime interest in law enforcement."

What the officers did was indicate their extent of agreement or disagreement (on a five-point scale) to eleven endings to the statement, "I entered policing due to. . . . " All six of the above reasons were given positive scores, but the remaining five reasons were rated negatively. That is, the officers *disagreed* that the following were reasons why they entered policing: salary/benefits, a friend/relative being an officer, authority/power of the job, lack of other job opportunities, and desire to be in a male-dominated occupation.

The officers also indicated agreement or disagreement with the same eleven reasons responding to the statement: "MEN enter policing due to . . . " and "WOMEN enter policing due to . . . " Here there were some interesting differences between the men and women. Not as far as the women's reasons were concerned. Everyone agreed women's top three reasons were to help people, job security and the excitement of the job.

Where women and men officers differed was in their perceptions of why men become police officers. While authority/power was ranked ninth by the men as a personal motivation (why *they* entered police work), the men ranked it sixth when thinking about other men. And the women said authority and power was *the number one reason* why men entered the police, in a tie with excitement of job. The women also departed from the men in their perception that men do become police officers to be in a male-dominated occupation. The men didn't agree with this.

Meagher and Yentes' research brings up the intriguing issue of which judgments to place more faith in. When describing ourselves, do we endorse the more socially desirable alternatives and reject the socially undesirable, regardless of the truth? And, when we have to say what motivates *other* people we know, in this case men police and women police as groups, are we closer to the mark? Especially when it comes to our own sex? Or the other sex?

Are men more attracted to police work because it is male-dominated and has authority and power than they admit for themselves? Are women likewise more attracted to police work because of the money than they admitted here? Speaking for themselves personally, Meagher and Yentes' women *disagreed* with salary/benefits as a motivation. It was seventh on their list. Yet the men said salary/benefits was the fourth most important reason for women and the women said it was fifth for other women.

Weisheit's (1987) results with 42 female and 191 male Illinois State police support Meagher and Yentes' conclusion that the job motivations of the sexes are quite close. And, that service to others and security for oneself are the top motivations of police today, with salary farther down the list.

The state police work primarily in rural areas, they rely greatly on single-officer patrols, and their primary function is patrol. They are considered elite among police organizations.

These Illinois state troopers ranked five reasons for entering policing. Because there were big age differences in their responses to Weisheit's survey, he limited his analysis to officers 30 years old or younger (44 men and 37 women). There are apparent differences between the motives of the sexes, but all were statistically *insignificant.* The primary motives of the men were security, 34 percent; service, 30 percent; excitement, 14 percent; status, 18 percent; and salary, 5 percent. The primary motives of the women were security, 19 percent; service, 43 percent; excitement, 16 percent; status, 11 percent; and salary, 11 percent.

The big age differences among these officers were important to take into account. For example, older officers are much more security minded than younger officers. Thus, if a much older group of men is compared to a much younger group of women (which is the way most groups studied are), we can be led, spuriously, to believe that men are not as service-oriented as women are today. Indeed, even though the above percentages give an edge to women in service motive (43 percent versus 30 percent), it is not a significant difference.

Motives are what get people into occupations, but job satisfaction keeps them there. How are women police faring?

WOMEN OFFICERS' JOB SATISFACTIONS

Donald Zytowski (1989) administered the Kuder Occupational Interest Survey (KOIS) to 348 members of the International Association of Women Police (IAWP) in 1987 in order to develop a women police scale for the KOIS. Such a scale allows counselees to see how closely their interests match those of women police and to use that information as a basis for exploring the police as a career.

In doing this research Zytowski asked the women officers, if they had the choice and were starting all over again, would they choose to be a (a) police officer, (b) police officer with certain stipulations, or (c) different occupation than police officer? He used this question to separate the participants into three job satisfaction groups. Those who would be a police officer again without any reservations are "satisfied." Those who would be a police officer again "if" certain conditions applied Zytowski typifies as "slightly dissatisfied." And those who would chose to be something else are "dissatisfied."

Only 12 percent were dissatisfied. One-third were "slightly dissatisfied," and the majority, 55 percent, were satisfied. I think we would have to conclude on the basis of this item that women police are reasonably well-satisfied with their jobs. It is against this general finding, then, that we will now look at what goes into satisfaction. Then we will return to Zytowski's study to get some insight into dissatisfaction.

A First IAWP Profile of Job Satisfaction

The best study so far having to do with the job satisfaction of women police was conducted with officers attending the 1986 Annual Conference of the International Association of Women Police in Denver, Colorado. Eric Poole and Mark Pogrebin, professors of criminal justice, report one of the best response rates for surveys on police, 80 percent (1988). The sample they concentrated on in their writeup was entirely nonranking, that is, 257 line-level women in state, local, or federal law enforcement agencies.

What Poole and Pogrebin were principally interested in were the women's rankings of eight factors important to their decision *to remain employed* as police officers. The women ranked the three they judged most important. Here are their results from the most to the least important factor based on the women's rankings:

1. Salary and/or benefits of the job
2. Challenge and excitement of police work
3. Job security
4. Job satisfaction
5. Enjoy working with people
6. Career advancement in law enforcement
7. Work relations with fellow officers
8. Need employment

Salary/benefits received the top ranking by 25 percent of the women and 70 percent of them selected salary/benefits as one of the three most important reasons for remaining in law enforcement. Similarly, challenge/

excitement was top ranked by 28 percent and over half of the women ranked it as one of their top three reasons.

In contrast, coworker relations was not among the top three reasons for 80 percent of the group and "need employment" was not among the top three for 92 percent. In fact, the authors feel that six of the eight factors were of little importance to the women judging from the considerably lower rankings of the six. Salary and benefits, challenge and excitement, were the whole story for this sample.

Poole and Pogrebin were also interested in how length of time in current rank in present department affected the women's judgments. Are different factors important at different stages in one's career? The way they phrased it was, once women face the range of career obstacles and have attempts to advance thwarted, do their reasons for staying change?

With the passage of time, going from less than three years on the job to over twelve years, four things happened. First, salary and benefits got more important. Second, so did job security. But career advancement became less and less important, until among those with 12 years of service, no one gave it as her top ranked reason to remain employed.

The fourth important trend over the years was that challenge/excitement stayed the same. At all stages of their careers these women police officers were motivated by the challenge and excitement of police work.

The saddest finding is surely what happened to the motivation of career advancement. It tied challenge and excitement as the first choice in the very youngest group. But after only three years, advancement was top ranked by only 7 percent. And in the group of women with over twelve years of service, it was most important to no one.

Why does advancement decline as a motive for women? Poole and Pogrebin speculate that it is because there are no role models in the highest ranks, and that women have plenty of time to see what happens to women supervisors—male resistance, greater stress, and lowered peer acceptance. They also speculate that one reason challenge and excitement continue to motivate women is because they have to constantly prove they are just as good as men. Women have a kind of built-in challenge that never goes away.

Other Studies of Women's Job Satisfaction

Two other studies highlight a major motivation for 1980s' research. Proving the competence of women police may no longer be an issue, but how to keep that competence, how to prevent attrition among women officers, definitely is an issue. Are their skills being utilized? Are their supervisors supportive? Does the job interfere with other responsibilities important to women?

To find ways to maintain levels of female utilization comparable to those of male officers, Garrison, Grant, and McCormick (1988) did another study with 180 IAWP members. My reading of the women's responses leaves me ambivalent as to whether they were more satisfied or more dissatisfied. On the one hand, only 45 percent said they were properly utilized, only 36 percent used all their skills on the job, and only 45 percent said they had the same opportunities as male officers for special assignments. A majority did *not* say "yes" to any of these important aspects to job satisfaction.

On the other hand, 87 percent said they would recommend law enforcement as a career for other women, and only 23 percent said they were considering a career change! Seventy-three percent said both that they would recommend the career *and* were not considering changing it. The 87 percent figure for those who would recommend the job to other women was considerably higher than for workers in general. Garrison et al. report a survey by the University of Michigan with a broad cross-section of American workers found only 62 percent would recommend their job to friends.

How do these researchers summarize their results? They feel the underutilization they observed may be due to four factors: overeducation; unfulfilled expectations among young women; limited variability in assignments (surprisingly, number of different assignments was not a function of years of service); and mismatch of job assignments and job preferences.

Certainly the lack of change in assignment was noticeable. Here we have a group, 79 percent of whom had been in policing five years or longer, and 47 percent reported they had had no change or just one change in assignment! Indeed, 82 percent had two or fewer changes in assignment. Variety in assignment is an important source of job satisfaction in women police and lack of variety in assignment is an important source of job *dissatisfaction,* particularly if a person has education, skills, and talents that can only be fully utilized through a range of different duties.

The authors also felt underutilization was related to a lack of synchronization between what the women preferred to do and what they had been assigned to. Only 13 percent preferred administrative services, yet 35 percent had been there. And only 6 percent preferred vice, while 14 percent had had that assignment, while 5 percent preferred juvenile, and 12 percent had been assigned it. Frankly, I found it gratifying that inasmuch as patrol was the first choice of 44 percent, 78 percent had actually had patrol experience for a median time of five years!

Other research that included job satisfaction questionnaire items was the Janus, Janus, Lord, and Power (1988) study with 135 women officers, whose service ranged from one year to 28 years, with 44 percent having served between 3–10 years.

To Janus et al. the best indicator of job satisfaction was the fact that 64 percent planned to stay in police work until retirement, compared to only 18 percent who said they would not. Another 18 percent were undecided. However, only 28 percent would encourage a daughter to become a police officer, and more, 36 percent, would *not* encourage her. Here 36 percent were undecided. Again, are women police more satisfied or more dissatisfied with their jobs? No wonder that classic book on policing, now edited by Elaine Niederhoffer and Abraham Blumberg, is titled *The Ambivalent Force*.

Comparing Women and Men Officers' Job Satisfaction

Although Mimi Silbert titled her 1982 article, "Job Stress and Burnout of New Police Officers" it also had a lot to say about job satisfaction. She had 216 men and 51 women officers with the San Francisco Police fill out a questionnaire that contained several questions about life and work. That these women were less satisfied with their jobs than the men can be seen from the women finding more positive features in their homelives than did the men, while the men had more positive features in their worklives. The women also had more negative features in their worklives than did the men, while the men reported more negative features in their homelives. Women's greater stress and burnout levels were indicated, Silbert felt, by a statistically significant greater intention to leave the police than men if offered another job at the same pay.

Fry and Greenfield (1980) studied five kinds of job attitudes in 529 male and 21 female first-line patrol officers in a large midwestern department. They didn't find any differences between the women and the men. Not in General Job Satisfaction. Not in Commitment to the

Organization. Not in Job-Induced Anxiety, Role Conflict, or Role Ambiguity.

Fry and Greenfield's findings are a lot like those discussed in the chapter on personality traits. Despite being in the minority, and despite the stress of male resistance, this sample of women responded as their male colleagues did to the questionnaire items having to do with staying awake at night worrying about the job, feeling fidgety because of the job, and thinking that a change of job might improve one's health.

Results similar to Fry and Greenfield's have been reported by Hunt, McCadden, and Mordaunt (1983) in a sample of 1,101 men and 68 women from six law enforcement agencies across the country. They found no sex differences in participants' responses to a mail questionnaire having to do with the goals of police work. The women agreed with the men in seeing themselves more as crime fighters than social workers. The women agreed with the men on the importance of such goals as providing emergency services, punishing lawbreakers, and protecting property. Both sexes were equally clear about their roles in achieving these goals. Both experienced the same degree of "role conflict," which had more to do with conflict with citizens and the courts than with conflict within the police community itself. Hunt et al. comment that while we will have to study more women to be certain, it appears that women who enter police work are no different from men in what they perceive their occupational roles to be.

Another study which compared men and women's job satisfaction is Weisheit's (1987) survey of Illinois State police. He asked the troopers to suppose that they had a *son* who wanted to go into policing and asked how much they would encourage him. Then they were to assume that they had a *daughter* who wanted to go into policing and say how much they would encourage her. Looking at amount of discouragement, 22 percent of the men, but only 14 percent of the women, would discourage a son, a difference which disappears when age is controlled. So Weisheit concluded the sexes are equally, moderately supportive of sons entering police work.

In contrast, when they thought about their daughters, 56 percent of the men would discourage them, but, again, only 14 percent of the women would discourage them. Here when age was controlled, the difference between the sexes did not go away. To me, this degree of support from women for their daughters reflects high job satisfaction.

Acknowledging that New Zealand is a different culture from the U.S.

and New Zealand police are undoubtedly under less stress than U.S. police, how do women and men officers there compare in job satisfaction? Love and Singer (1988) studied 103 male and 75 female police officers from Christchurch, Wellington, and Auckland using both a general job satisfaction measure and specific job satisfaction scales. There were no differences at all between the women and the men.

They were equally satisfied in general, for example, responding similarly to an item which referred to thoughts about quitting. They were equally satisfied with five aspects to satisfaction: pay and fringe benefits, job security, the social benefits of the job (both from coworkers and from helping other people), supervision, and personal growth and challenge.

Looking at the mean scores on the specific scales, both women and men alike were least satisfied with their pay and most satisfied with their job security.

WOMEN OFFICERS' JOB DISSATISFACTION

If women like police work, if they're generally satisfied despite the stresses, then why do they leave? For the same reasons men do? Or for completely different reasons? What lies behind women's dissatisfaction with the police?

Radelet (1986) in reviewing earlier job dissatisfaction data noted the high percentage of women (54 percent) and men (46 percent of whites, 52 percent of blacks) who got into police work by accident after trying out several other jobs. Even though policing turned out, for the majority, to be different from what they had imagined, 80 percent had given little or no thought to leaving. Their chief job satisfaction was security; their chief job dissatisfactions were lack of advancement, lack of pay, and too much paper work.

Now for some recent data. Zytowski's (1989) major study on the vocational interests of women police, as I noted earlier in this chapter, included a job satisfaction item. If they were starting over again, would they choose to be a police officer unqualified, or a police officer under certain conditions, or not to be a police officer?

Those checking that they'd choose a different occupation were defined by Zytowski as "dissatisfied" with their jobs. They numbered only 42, 12 percent of the sample, and while we do not know the source of their dissatisfaction, we can say these things about them.

Dissatisfaction had nothing to do with years in the police service. For the whole group of 348, 1–3 years experience were reported by 17 percent; 4–6 years by 17 percent; 7–10 years by 31 percent; 11–15 years by 24 percent; and 11 percent had 16 or more years experience. There was no hint that dissatisfaction was related to either lack of experience or too many years in the service.

Likewise the number of previous jobs held was not related to dissatisfaction. For the total group, 8 percent had no previous jobs, 33 percent one job, 25 percent two jobs, and 34 percent had held 3 or more jobs prior to becoming police officers.

Was dissatisfaction associated with rank? I sorted the women into two groups based on ranks. The lower level group consisted of all the patrol officers, troopers, investigator/detectives, and deputy sheriffs. They accounted for 62 percent of the sample. The higher level group consisted of four ranks: corporal/sergeant, lieutenant/captain, special agent, and ranks such as deputy U.S. marshall, major, deputy inspector, chief, sheriff. Just as with years experience and number of jobs previously held, rank was not related to job satisfaction.

Do race or age have any relationship to dissatisfaction? Not in this sample. In terms of racial composition, 91 percent of the group was white, 4 percent black, and 5 percent other minorities. Eighteen percent of the total group was under 30, 40 percent were between 30 and 35, and 42 percent were 36 and over.

We can get some clues to dissatisfaction, however, from looking at the conditions placed upon choosing to be a police officer by those 116 women who were "slightly dissatisfied." Here are the percentages who checked each of the eight conditions provided by Zytowski (they won't add up to 100 because they could check all that applied):

More opportunity for advancement	51
Better pay	46
A better image outside the profession	39
Better supervision	34
More chance for creativity	33
Greater opportunity to be of help to people	23
Better relations with co-workers	20
Better chance to supervise others	18

The women could also write in other reasons. Dissatisfaction with sexism in the department was the overall theme in these additional reasons. They wanted greater acceptance and not having to live up to a super-macho stereotype. They resented favoritism and nepotism. But primarily they wanted "equal advancement with male officers," "equal performance standards," and an end to discrimination by administrative staff. They also wanted greater freedom to relocate and move laterally, better hours, and greater understanding given injured officers.

Fry's (1983) study also supports the idea that job dissatisfaction is primarily based on lack of advancement opportunity. He studied the personnel records of 29 women and 261 men police officers who had left a California county sheriff's department over a nine year period. The men and women differed in three important ways. One, the women who quit were of lower rank than the men. Ninety-three percent of the women were deputies versus 78 percent of the men. Two, 72 percent of the women as opposed to 27 percent of the men had jail assignments when they quit. And three, more women than men left to accept employment with other law enforcement agencies.

Interviews with the women revealed that their continued assignment in the women's jail made them feel they would never get the patrol experience they needed to get promoted. So they left for other departments where they could be on patrol and eventually advance (or be on day shift so that they could take care of their families).

TURNOVER: JOB DISSATISFACTION
OR FAMILY RESPONSIBILITIES?

I should be able to start this discussion by quoting current statistics on the turnover of women police compared to men police. But I cannot for a very simple reason. After 1981 the Bureau of Labor Statistics, due to severe budgetary cutbacks, ended its surveys of labor turnover. Everything that can be found, however, suggests attrition rates for women police are slightly higher than rates for men police.

This is what Horne (1980) concluded. He quoted a 1974 national rate of 11.6 percent for women and 10.4 percent for men. And he noted that studies both in California and St. Louis City and County in the 1970s reported a higher turnover rate for females than males.

If we allow ourselves to generalize from U.K. women police to our own, there are good data from Great Britain. Sandra Jones (1986) provides early turnover rates for men and women officers from 1971 to 1982. The women's rates are all four or five times higher than the men's rates. The rates, however, seem to be falling for both sexes. In 1971 the percentage of women with premature turnover was 12.9 percent, men 2.2 percent. In 1982 the women's rate was 7.6 percent, the men's 1.5 percent (p. 92).

Turnover rates are often used as an index of job dissatisfaction. But if women police have greater turnover than men, should we necessarily conclude it is because they are more dissatisfied with their jobs?

The experts who write about women's attrition suggest it has little to do with job dissatisfaction. Women leave because police work is very difficult to mesh with meeting family responsibilities, and most women do desire to have a family. This was Horne's (1980, p. 137) presumption and also Jones' (1986, p. 127). They say it is not a matter of lack of commitment or having different job motivation than men. British and American women leave policing prematurely to have families.

Martin (1980) presents evidence that when they start work, women do not *expect* to resign from the police in any greater proportions than men do. Exactly the same proportion (22 percent) of the 28 women and 27 men officers she studied said they expected to move to another occupation within five years (p. 70). On the other hand, Martin presents a complex of reasons why the women were more likely to leave than the men. Security, medical benefits, and retirement were far less important to this group of women. They stayed for the money and because they liked the work, but they were much more pessimistic about promotion than the men. But the most important factor was that their career expectations were contingent on what else might happen in their lives, marriage and family responsibilities. In contrast, none of the men expected family or personal circumstances to affect their careers (pp. 69–75).

RECAP

Just as in days of old, the motives of service to others and job security are high on officers' lists of motivations for policing. The difference today is *both* are high on *both* women's and men's lists.

Salary is also important, but probably secondary to service and security as a motive, but salary and job benefits certainly are chief sources of job satisfaction once women are in the police.

The challenge and excitement of police work are also a primary job motive and job satisfaction, factors that do not wax or wane over time.

Most women officers would, if starting all over again, still choose the police as a career. Which is not to say they are totally satisfied with it. Lack of women's advancement is clearly a problem, as is lack of variety in assignments. Men leave, too, because advancement prospects are limited and modern notions of "lateral promotion" lag. But women may leave primarily to raise families, while men seldom do.

The entire system, therefore, women, men, administrators, must ask itself: In fact, is the job of police officer not compatible with having a family? What adjustments can be made so that both men and women can have a satisfying family life and do a good job as a police officer besides? The experts have proposed a host of modifications that should be considered: part-time work, extended leaves with guaranteed rehiring, support for daycare. If the system wishes to retain its women, it is not that the job itself needs more challenge. The challenge is in meshing the satisfactions of police work with the satisfactions of the rest of life.

Chapter 7

STRESS AND COPING

How dangerous is the job of police officer? More dangerous than being a cab driver, flight attendant, or surveyor's helper, surely. No. In fact, all three of these jobs have more deaths per 100,000 people than does the job of police officer. In fact, police and detectives with 17.5 deaths per 100,000 ranked 24th among blue-collar jobs in dangerousness (Ubell, 1989). Loggers, insulation workers, and power-line repairers have three or more times as many on-the-job deaths as police officers.

Still, it's clear, even if the dangers are sometimes exaggerated, that law enforcement is a high stress occupation. And it is also clear from the research data we have so far, that lack of peer acceptance makes law enforcement more stressful for women than men.

Brenda Washington (1981, p. 142) points out how peer acceptance— being thought of as a "good officer"—bolsters and supports an officer's esteem and confidence and operates as a stress reducer to anger, abuse, and hostility from the outside. Because a woman (a rookie especially) has a much harder time earning that acceptance, the job is more stressful and frustrating for her. Even when she has the support of family and friends. Minority women have the extra burden of dealing with racial as well as sexual prejudice.

Washington says, as far as stress is concerned, the popular myth that women are weaker is opposite the biological facts (p. 144). The fact is that alcoholism and drug addiction are several times more prevalent among men than women. The fact is that men cope far less effectively to loss of spouse than women, even though women are more economically dependent on their spouses. Contrary to popular opinion, women do possess the physical and psychological make-up to endure long working hours, lack of sleep, disruption of family life, and all the other stresses of policing at least as well as men.

This chapter is concerned with the content of women's stressors and their level of stress compared to men, as well as with their personal coping strategies and responses to organizational attempts to reduce

93

women officers' stress. In the absence of research-based findings on how women officers and their departments can help them reduce stress, expert opinion is offered.

CONTENT OF WOMEN'S STRESSORS

"Sources of Stress among Women Police Officers," a 1983 article by Judie Wexler and Deana Logan, is a good introduction to the topic of stress in the police. There are basically four sources of stress in police work: external, organizational, task-related, and personal. Three examples of each are: *external* —negative public attitudes, media, the courts; *organizational* —poor pay, inadequate training, rumors; *task-related* —exposure to tragedy, danger to self, boredom; *personal* —lack of recognition, health problems, alcohol/drug concerns.

For women officers, however, these four sources of stress are not the whole story. Wexler and Logan had to add a fifth category, *female-related stressors.* They placed four stressors in this category: negative attitudes of male officers, group blame, responses of other men, and lack of role models.

Underscoring the importance of *female-related stressors* is the fact that they were three of the six most common stressors found in the 25 women Wexler and Logan studied over a 9-month period. The three female-related stressors among the top six were the negative attitudes of male officers, minority group blame, and the negative responses of men whom women police meet socially. The other three commonest stressors for women officers were training, rumors, and exposure to tragedy. Wexler and Logan say, however, even "training" and "rumors," stressors shared with men, were more painful for women officers.

What "group blame," which troubled 12 of the 25 women, means is the sense of being treated as a group and affected by the actions of all the other people in that group. Thus, the women worried that if another woman performed inadequately, the men would take that as proof that no woman, including themselves, could be a good police officer.

Stress from the negative attitudes of men police was reported by 80 percent of the women. There was both official harassment and individual harassment. Examples of official harassment were having no separate locker room facilities and being locked out of the station. Among the varieties of individual harassment were questions about the women's sexual orientation, refusal to talk to women officers, and blatant anti-women comments.

Glaser and Saxe (1982), who have worked with women going through the Los Angeles Police Departments' Crime Prevention Assistance Program (CPA), list six psychological stressors unique to women. (1) Doubts about competence and self-worth doing a traditional man's job; (2) Lack of support from men on and off the job; (3) Necessity to develop greater assertiveness and authority in voice and stature; (4) Inappropriate expectations regarding physical training, odd hours, and quasi-military environment; (5) Inability to work a 15-hour a day recruit schedule and also maintain a home; (6) Necessity to develop new defense mechanisms for stress, more appropriate to law enforcement.

Schwartz and Schwartz (1981) have discussed female-related stressors as well, and underlying all of them, they say, was lack of support. Women were subjected to greater testing from the men. They received little peer support. They received little middle management or supervisory support. Their agencies typically provided no programs through which they could receive assistance. As a result, the pressures which befell the typical white male, Schwartz and Schwartz say, were dwarfed by the pressures faced by minority and women officers.

LEVEL OF WOMEN'S STRESSORS

Now we know something about the content of women's stressors. What about level? Might not the overall stress of women police be higher than that of men because of the additional stress of the men themselves? For example, how much does it add to one's stress level to have men go right on believing that women aren't strong or aggressive enough, no matter how competently one performs?

Silbert (1982) studied stress in 216 men and 51 women police officers who had been in the San Francisco Police Department from one to five years. She found the women who filled out her survey were slightly more stressed by police work than the men. The women's average burnout score was higher than that of the men. Out of 21 physical symptoms asked about, the women experienced eleven. The men experienced only four. The women felt more physically exhausted and irritated than the men. They had more headaches, backaches, stomach aches and sleeping problems.

Silbert says the extra stress reported by the women resulted from the additional burden of negative attitudes from male coworkers. Part of this negativism was not giving women the social support men gave one another. The greatest sources of stress in this study, incidentally, were poor pay and frustration with the courts.

Silbert's women indicated more positive features in their lives *outside* of work than did men, while the men had more positive features *in their lives at work.* The same pattern held for negative features in one's life: the women had more negatives at work, the men more negatives away from work. This suggests to me that a woman's home and family, while a source of conflict over roles, are more effective as stress reducers than they are for men.

Pendergrass and Ostrove (1984) found evidence that women officers' stress level may be higher than men's even *without* the additional stress of negative male attitudes. They studied 352 male officers and 31 female officers in Montgomery County, Maryland, using an 11-page question-naire about the health consequences of job stress.

Women officers, together with women nonsworn civilian employees, suffered more physiological stress consequences than their male counter-parts — more headaches, muscle tension, nausea and upset stomach, and chest pain tension. Was this because the women experienced the *same* job events as *more* stressful than the men? For example, women officers rated as more stressful than men officers these stressful job events: killing someone in the line of duty, exposure to dead and battered children, not enough manpower to handle the job, physical attacks on one's person, making arrests alone, and responding to a felony in progress.

Men officers rated as more stressful than women two career issues: competition for advancement and changing shift hours. Thus, women's total stress was less due to worries over promotion and hours, and more about personal safety issues.

Pendergrass and Ostrove wanted to make the point that there was a strong relationship between the amount of stress from events such as these and the degree of *physiological* consequences reported. There was also a strong correlation between amount of job stress and the degree of *psychological* consequences reported. Psychological consequences were reactions such as sloppiness on the job, insomnia, cynicism, isolation from fellow employees, and a low opinion of oneself. In the psychologi-cal arena, however, the women experienced no more consequences than the men.

Davis' (1984) survey of 2,148 nonminority men and 145 women municipal police in Texas and Oklahoma asked participants to rate the degree of job-related stress they experienced. The women's rating of their general job-related stress didn't differ from the men's, for example, 62 percent of the men experienced "high" stress compared to 59 percent of the women. However, the women perceived danger as one of the main causes of stress in police work significantly more often than did the men, comparable to what Pendergrass and Ostrove found.

Davis felt women are "bound to feel more endangered" because they are physically disadvantaged dealing with angry, potentially violent citizens. But another item in Davis' survey suggests that what women lack may also be psychological. These women did not have the high degree of self-confidence the men felt as police officers. The women rated themselves the same as the men in feelings of "general effectiveness," but far fewer women felt *extremely self-confident* compared to the men.

Women Supervisors' Special Stresses

It has been suggested that women police in supervisory positions will experience greater male resistance, stress, and lower peer acceptance than lower-ranking women (Poole and Pogrebin, 1988). This is a hypothesis for future research. The only study I could find on stress and women supervisors asked this question: Do women police executives suffer additional stresses as they try to sensitize employees to what sexual harassment and sex-role stereotypes and sexism are all about?

Mariette Christophe's (1988) article on "Androgynous Management" describes the developmental process a woman police executive goes through as she tries to manage androgynously and the different stress that each phase brings with it. In Phase One, the woman executive is aware of the unconscious, unsatisfactory, sexist behavior many men display toward women. The stress of this awareness results in fatigue and depression.

In Phase Two, the woman police executive starts to feel angry as she watches traditional sex role behaviors being played out and sees no one else cares. In Phase Three, the executive deals with her stress by projecting her anger toward male colleagues. They, in turn, become even more aggressive. In Phase Four, men, who are now engaging in "*conscious,* unsatisfactory" sexist behavior, wish everything would get back to the old familiar rules of traditional sex-roles. The way to cope with stress in Phase Four, Christophe advises, is to talk to other women.

What this "emancipating manager" is working toward through these difficult, stressful phases is creating a workplace in which men and women engage in "consciously satisfactory" behavior (and ultimately, "*unconsciously* satisfactory" behavior) in their relationships to one another. So in Phase Five, when the manager sees that men and women are behaving consciously in a nonsexist fashion toward one another, her energies can now go to making other constructive changes in the organization. And at this stage, her stress level goes down because *she* is free to use the complementary traits of both sexes to manage truly androgynously.

WOMEN'S COPING STRATEGIES

Do women and men police cope with stress differently? Equally effectively? If women are made to feel that crying is an inappropriate stress reducer, what other techniques work for them?

Mary Cooper (1985), divorced mother of five and a sergeant in a university police department, said support from all directions was how she coped with stress. Her parents and children were her most avid supporters. She also began relying on the brotherhood of men officers during training where she described her fellow classmates as treating her as a mother and coming to her for advice on how to deal with wife, girlfriend, mother-in-law, and new baby problems. She said at *her* academy, "encouragement was neverending." Since then, seeking positive reinforcement and support has been her coping strategy. She got it from her immediate family and male colleagues, from a chief with whom she can discuss personal or professional problems, and from a major who tells her regularly not to lose her sense of humor.

Two big differences Ellison and Genz (1983) observed in the way women and men officers deal differently with stress have to do with emotional expressiveness on the job, and disclosures to spouses away from the job. When women feel upset after an acute crisis, they are more comfortable with their feelings and see the expression of emotion as not reflecting badly on their capability to do the job (p. 103). As far as disclosing what happens on the job to loved ones, Ellison and Genz say that men typically do not *tell* their wives about the job, while women commonly make disclosures to their husbands (p. 71).

Some Research Results

Judie Wexler (1985) says the amount of stress women police receive from male colleagues depends on how they relate to the men. Wexler describes three styles used in interacting with men officers: neutral-impersonal, semimasculine, and feminine.

Does the way a woman officer relates to men determine the amount of stress she is subjected to? Or is her style of interaction a coping strategy for handling the stresses imposed by male colleagues? Wexler's observations support a "yes" to both questions.

Neutral-impersonal style women received the most stress from the men. This style comes from trying to prove themselves as professionals. And in addition to receiving more stress from male coworkers, these women lacked an informal work group after working hours which is a good stress reducer.

In contrast, women whose style was either semimasculine or feminine were less stressed. Semimasculine women socialized with men after work and didn't mind being teased. Feminine women flirted and let men help them. In return, both groups received support, acceptance, and protection, of a sort, from the men. However, while these styles were effective at reducing stress, they cost the semimasculine and feminine women professional recognition from the men.

Thirty-four men and 19 women officers attending a crime seminar responded to a questionnaire having to do with stress symptoms and coping strategies (Martin, McKean, and Veltkamp, 1986). The worst stresses in terms of symptoms such as sleep disturbances and hyperalertness were having one's own family threatened and working with rape victims. The women differed significantly from the men in their use of talk with fellow officers to cope with stress. Ninety percent of the women talked out their sources of stress versus 45 percent of the men. A large number of stresses were reported by more women than men, while more men than women said they had none at all.

Having one's own family threatened brings up the notion that police work not only means working with victims but feeling a victim oneself or seeing one's family victimized by one's work. The authors feel that women officers are exposed to more traumas with which they identify emotionally, such as working with rape victims. The women did report feeling empathetic with rape victims more often than did the men.

These authors say that women's coping profile—talking to other officers, talking to family, trying to forget their stress—showed that women more openly feel and deal with the stress of working with victims and being victims themselves of their work. The authors reflect that men reporting less exposure to stress can't be due to their *actually* being exposed to less stress. Was it due to the fact that the men were older and had had more time to develop the strategy of emotionally distancing themselves from trauma? Or was it because it is culturally more acceptable for women to report stress and to look for help and support?

Expert Advice for the Individual

Brenda Washington (1981), an expert on how to deal with stress, has offered women officers five guidelines for reducing stress which are paraphrased below. A woman police officer should:

1. Prior to becoming a police officer decide *what is morally right and wrong for her personally* and see if that coincides with police codes and policies.

2. Not judge her job performance by anyone else's *standards* but *her own.*

3. Accept and *cope with the consequences* of her actions even when those consequences are unfair and she doesn't like them.

4. Keep *a few quality friends* from the past.

5. Accept that the *job will affect every aspect of her life adversely,* the degree of adversity depending on how flexible she is and how accepting significant others are.

Lucille Bell (1988) listed seven ways to short circuit stress overload. Women officers will especially appreciate number six. Again, paraphrasing. . . .

1. Take the time to be introspective and think about what you want from life as an individual and a family member.

2. Talk to the people who live with you.

3. Be creative with your free time and plan new activities and hobbies.

4. Develop new friendships through various activities and organizations.

5. Participate in a physical exercise program.

6. Let different family members be responsible for planning and cooking meals. Add new foods to your diet.

7. Learn biofeedback and relaxation techniques. Attend stress seminars.

ORGANIZATIONAL ATTEMPTS TO REDUCE WOMEN'S STRESS

Carol Ann Martin (1983) emphasized the added stress of negative attitudes from male colleagues. It may consist of the stress of constantly trying to prove you're as good as a man, or overcompensating for less qualified women who were hired just to fill quotas. Or it may be constant anti-women remarks, or demeaning discriminatory acts such as not being trusted to drive a squad car.

While Martin counsels women to reduce stress through diet, exercise, and positive thinking, she also recommends that police organizations provide various kinds of training to help women deal with stress. She suggests self-defense training, assertiveness training, stress management, and training in psychology and how to supervise. What do we know about the success of organizational efforts such as these?

The Efforts of the LAPD

Between 1976 and 1980, Alan Kerstein (1982) reports, more than 50 percent of women candidates to the Los Angeles Police Department (LAPD) did not graduate from the police academy, while the failure rate for men was 17 percent. However, in 1980 only 17 percent of women candidates who had participated in LAPD's Crime Prevention Assistant (CPA) program failed to graduate, and the goal for 1981 was to get the failure rate down to 15 percent. What went into this program to give women an equal chance to survive the academy as men recruits?

While the primary component of the CPA program was physical, according to Kerstein, that is, calisthenics, running, and weight training to develop upper body strength, other components were aimed at reducing stress. The women received group and individual counseling on how to handle sexual harassment and the pressures of the police lifestyle. They also received Power Orientation for Winning Response (POWR) training, a kind of assertiveness training for handling stress and its causes in a very personal manner. The women were taught how to analyze stress, relaxation techniques, and other strategies for dealing with stress. The idea was to teach that stress was an artificial barrier to success and to give each woman confidence that she could perform physically in the face of stressful circumstances.

Debra Glaser and Susan Saxe (1982) have also described the CPA program. They emphasize its psychological component, that is, POWR training and group counseling. About POWR training, they say these sessions are presented daily for an hour immediately prior to physical training. Audio tapes designed specifically for the program are played. They present progressive relaxation instructions and suggestions for imagining the successful completion of a task, such as chinups and long runs, or the proud feelings of graduation day.

CPA's group counseling consisted of weekly 2-hour sessions over a period of 4 to 6 weeks. During these sessions the women identified their stressors, shared information on the realities of police work, and discussed their feelings in an atmosphere of confidentiality. They also role-played scenarios on and off the job, as a preview of how they might respond not only as police officers, but as wives trying to explain police work to husbands and families. It was hoped that the cohesiveness and mutual support developed in group counseling would transfer to the academy training situation so that the women would succeed in greater numbers. Glaser and Saxe also report a dramatic drop in attrition between 1980 and 1981 due to this additional "psychological preparation."

Expert Advice for the Organization

Elsewhere in this book we talk about how police training has been, or could be, modified because officers are now both women and men. One might suppose the introduction of women would mean solely softening and civilizing training. However, the following advice from a woman concerned about helping other women cope with stress is quite the opposite of humanizing the rigors of the academy. Her advice to police academies may be controversial. See what you think.

Brenda Washington (1981) suggests that in the course of doing routine tasks academy instructors engage in the following behaviors to achieve specific, stress-reducing results among women recruits.

1. Instructors should emphasize superior-inferior relationships between themselves and recruits. From this women learn the semi-military nature of police procedures.

2. Instructors should be loud and harsh in discipline. From this women get used to the verbal abuse they will encounter on the street.

3. Instructors should punish mistakes with strenuous physical training. In this way women build greater physical and emotional endurance.

4. Instructors should require recruits, at regular intervals, to perform at maximum capacity. Again, women gain endurance.

5. Instructors should periodically require women to take command of a class. This will develop the leadership skills and confidence women need on the street.

6. Instructors should put women and men together in stressful and not stressful situations in which they must work together to accomplish a goal. This is to give women perspective on the simple fact that men achieve male peer acceptance much more easily than women do.

7. Instructors should put women in stressful situations where they must think and act for themselves. Again, the goal is greater confidence.

8. Instructors should put recruits through mock courtroom dramas. Thus women will overcome their fears of testifying in court before they must actually do so.

FUTURE PROSPECTS FOR RESEARCH

How are female-related stressors changing with time? Are men officers just as negative in 1990 as they were in 1980? Are women as concerned today with being blamed for the inadequacies of other women? Are civilian men better able to cope with girlfriends who carry guns? Are there enough women officers now that lack of role models no longer counts as a female-related stressor? Does the disappearance of female-related stressors bring the level of women officers' stress down to that of men?

Does the fact of women and men working together result in each sex teaching the other new ways to cope with stress? What departmental programs aimed at stress reduction for both sexes have been successful — prior to training, in training, on the job, and for the job of supervisor?

Chapter 8

PERFORMANCE AND STYLE OF POLICING

E valuation studies comparing women's and men's performance were a phenomenon of the 1970s. Since then, research articles and the references cited by those articles, in publications such as *Police Chief*, *Police Studies*, and the *Journal of Police Science and Administration*, indicate that big police departments are no longer funding studies to assess women officers' effectiveness.

In one sense, this comes as no surprise. The evaluation studies did not demonstrate that women could not do the job, so the best thing for reluctant police organizations to do was accept this fact and start hiring women. It was the law, after all, that there should be no sex discrimination in hiring or employment. For departments enthusiastic about women changing the police image to one of responsiveness and understanding, likewise, why do more performance studies? Thus, to resistant and progressive departments alike, more evaluation may have appeared a waste of time and money.

But what has come as a surprise to me is the lack of studies in the 1980s devoted to the topic of women's and men's different styles of policing. Few people, in or out of the police, believe that there are absolutely no differences in the way the sexes go about the job.

For example, Milton et al. (1974), who are insiders to the police system, summarize the key findings of the St. Louis County, Missouri evaluation entirely in terms of sex differences. Women performed in a less aggressive fashion, citizens said women handled service and domestic calls better, there was less likelihood of escalation of potentially violent situations with women than men. Women had the edge in public contacts and community relations, but men had the edge in accepting responsibility and initiative, and in making arrests and engaging in preventive activities.

Similarly, journalist Tom Seligman (1985), who is outside the system, concluded from his interviews across the country that women officers have a less aggressive, more calming, nonconfrontational style. Women are more gentle, polite, and compassionate; they use talk more and nightsticks less.

Some people believe these sex differences are slight, others that they are large, others that they are small but significant. Some people believe women's style is more effective overall, others that men's style is superior. But almost everyone believes in these sex differences. It's a puzzle, then, why there have not been more studies in the 1980s devoted to style differences in policing.

If big police departments are no longer doing evaluation studies, however, performance is still a worthy subject for graduate students with criminal justice interests.

RECENT PERFORMANCE DATA

The kind of study that is done today which allows us to compare women and men officers' effectiveness is represented by Catherine Jones' master's thesis (1987a) titled "Predicting the Effectiveness of Police Officers." Jones (1987b) has made additional unpublished analyses on her data available for this book, providing an update to the large-scale performance studies of the 1970s.

Jones studied 230 men and 55 women officers with the San Diego Police Department. About half of the sample had gone through the academy in 1979 and 1980, the other half graduated in 1985. They had worked for the Department for 1–7 years. Jones' data were entirely archival.

Jones had 11 measures of job performance. Seven of them were supervisor's (sergeant) most recent performance ratings on a five-point scale: 1, unsatisfactory; 2, improvement needed; 3, satisfactory; 4, highly satisfactory; and 5, superior. The seven ratings were:

1. Overall—general assessment.
2. Performance—included self-initiated activity, report writing, driving skills, investigative ability, judgment, dependability, composure and stress control, observation skills, teamwork, verbal communication.
3. Attitude—attitude towards police work, acceptance of criticism, self-image, confidence, and demeanor.
4. Knowledge—of department guidelines, codes, procedures, techniques.
5. Job readiness—included personal appearance, proper forms and equipment, degree informed on crime and community problems, and participation in squad conferences.

6. Physical abilities—included use of sick leave, strength/condition, and coordination/agility.

7. Leadership—technical support, training others, acceptance of responsibility, acceptance by others, and leadership ability.

In addition to these seven ratings, performance was also measured by numbers of commendations, reprimands, and days suspended. The eleventh measure for officers no longer employed by the department was the recommendation to rehire.

These San Diego women and men officers differed on only one of the eleven performance measures, number 5, job readiness, men having an average rating of 3.3 to the women's 3.1. One would have to conclude, as the 1970s evaluation studies did, that women and men are equally effective as police officers.

Jones also has made available other performance data indirectly related to later on-the-job effectiveness. She gathered academy scores in eleven academy courses, plus final academy score, final physical agilities test score, field training summary score, and "rephase" score (whether or not the recruit was placed back into field training for additional instruction after 12 weeks).

The eleven courses were in Laws of Arrest, Crime Scene Preservation and the Collection of Evidence, Report Writing, Sex Crimes, Vehicle Stops, Unusual Circumstances, Crime Prevention, Patrol Theory and Method, Arrest and Control, First Aid, and Criminal Law. It is important to note that "Arrest and Control" scores were a combination of two *barely* correlated scores, one a written test score and the other a highly subjective rating of performance. Physical Agilities scores, which could range from 0 to 20, were based on pullups and situps in a specified time period, a routine on apparatus bars, and how fast an individual runs 440 yards.

Jones reports that the sexes did not differ on ten of these 15 academy measures, but on five they did. Four of the five significant differences were quite small, a function of the relatively large sample sizes.

Although their final overall percentile academy scores were 92 for the men and 91 for the women, the difference is statistically significant. Similarly, men's percentile score of 88 was significantly higher than the women's 85 in Criminal Law, as was the men's average Field Training Sum of 12 compared to the women's of 11. But where the women and men clearly differed was in Physical Agilities scores—12 versus 6—and in the proportions which had to be "rephased" back into the field for more patrol experience. Only 9 percent of the men were rephased but 24 percent of the women were.

One might be tempted to dismiss differences in the ability to do pullups and run 440 yards, but these performance differences were extremely important in that Physical Agilities, for whatever reason, was the best single predictor of those eleven measures of job performance listed above!

Jones feels supervisors may unconsciously give higher performance evaluations to people who look and act physically fit. If this is so, women should realize the importance of maintaining physical agility. It can have a positive "halo effect" when it comes to their job proficiency ratings.

MORE ABOUT PHYSICAL AGILITY

The ninetieth class of the Michigan State Police Training Academy held in 1977 provided the data for Michael Charles (1981) to study women and men recruits' academic, technical, and physical performances, as well as their peer evaluations of one another and perceptions of the female trooper's role.

There were 50 males and 14 females in the class which lasted 12 weeks. Only 9 percent of them had just a high school education. The rest had attended college, held a degree, or had done graduate work. Seventy percent were white, 19 percent black, and 11 percent "other."

Academy records provided the objective data which showed that the women and men were equally successful in their academic courses and their technical courses. Academic courses such as criminal law and court functions depended on traditional learning skills. Technical courses such as water safety and precision driving required mechanical skills.

The third area of learning at the academy was physical: defensive tactics and boxing. Here the data were purely subjective, that is, ratings of physical ability and aggressiveness at defensive tactics and boxing done by four Michigan State Police personnel.

How did the women compare to the men? They did significantly more poorly on their physical ability scores, primarily in defensive tactics. However, on physical aggressiveness there were no significant differences between the men and women.

Charles commented that there were two kinds of male recruits, those who gained respect for the women's aggressiveness in the boxing ring and those who used the boxing ring to prove that women cannot perform equally with men in physical confrontations. Charles also commented that the women, without exception and without looking for favoritism, undertook boxing with "fervor and determination." Their willingness to continue matches after being knocked to the mat and to keep fighting aggressively won the approval of many men.

These recruits bring to mind a story told in Bryna Taubman's *Lady Cop* (1987, p. 59). An instructor with a sick sense of humor paired a five foot tall, 100 pound woman with one of the biggest men. She didn't complain about her sparring partner, she just climbed into the ring. In less than a minute the man was down, and the woman's hands were over her head in a victory gesture. So the instructor sent another guy into the ring, almost as big as the first. A minute later, he was down. A third partner was set up for her and in two minutes he, too, was on the mat. Turns out she was the sparring partner for her four brothers who fought the Golden Gloves. But she had more than practice. She had her own unique style of coming up from underneath, on tiptoe, to deliver her knockdown punches.

USING WEAPONS

Janus, Janus, Lord, and Power (1988) asked 135 women police how confident they were that they could use force in a violent or potentially violent situation. Thirty-two percent said they were capable "with some reservations," but 62 percent had no reservations. They were physically and emotionally able to respond with force. Had they ever used force in a violent case? Twenty-three percent said no, 77 percent said yes. Only 3 percent, however, had ever shot a suspect.

Grennan (1987) set out to test three assumptions he felt some police officials make about female officers in violent encounters with citizens. Police executives, he surmised, believe that (1) female-male patrols have more injuries than male-male patrols during violent confrontations due to general female incompetence, (2) female officers, because they lack stature and strength, resort to discharging firearms more than male officers during violent confrontations, and (3) male officers in mixed patrols get injured more often than female officers because the women stand around in the background and consequently don't get hurt.

Grennan analyzed the 3,073 violent confrontations experienced by patrol teams in 1983 in New York City to test his three hypotheses. Over

150 predictors of injuries to patrol teams were studied, including the gender of the team. Injuries were positively related to several of Grennan's predictors. For example, incidents which initially appeared less overtly threatening, turned out to be associated with more injuries. *But injuries were not related to the gender of the teams.*

Further, in answer to the other hypotheses, in mixed gender teams, males discharged firearms significantly *more often* than their female partners and had the *same* number of injuries as the women, not more. Grennan concluded that female officers use the same style of reacting to violent confrontations that men use. But it is important to remember that the women in this sample used their guns less. A big style difference.

Blumberg (1985) working in Kansas City reported an extensive analysis of the relationship between officer characteristics and shootings. He looked at 10 officer characteristics: age, length of police service, race, social class, height, marital status at appointment, military service, pre-service firearms experience, prior arrest record, and sex. The only officer characteristics related to shooting behavior were age and length of police service. Younger and less experienced officers were more likely to get involved in shootings.

While sex was not significantly related to shooting behavior, Blumberg says there was "some evidence" that women are less likely to shoot at citizens, but he says until greater numbers of female officers are studied, we won't know for sure.

STRENGTHS AND LIMITATIONS

Despite the number and range of data-gathering instruments used in the 1974 Bloch and Anderson evaluation study (observations, files, surveys, interviews, ratings, etc.), the principal differences between the women and men turned out to be just three: the women made fewer arrests and gave fewer traffic citations, the men more often engaged in serious unbecoming conduct, and the women got more light duty due to injuries, although their injuries did not cause them to be absent from work more often than the men. These conclusions lead one to suspect that while there may well be major style differences in women and men officers' behavior, in the end, both sexes get the same job done.

However, women's advocates such as Peter Horne (1980), in trying to win police administrators over to the view that women should do everything in policing that men do, emphasized that women's understanding, gentleness, empathy, and nonaggressive approach make them especially useful *outside* general patrol. Where women's style is most valuable to the organization is in the areas of community relations, communications, crime prevention, juvenile work, and traffic analysis. Women possess the bona fide occupational qualification for doing searches of women in the field and in jail, as well as the BFOQ to act as decoys for men in search of a prostitute. And while men can be trained to be as sensitive as women with rape victims, women should be available for rape victims who prefer to talk to women (pp. 78–89).

Diane Pike (1985) spent nine weeks at one police academy and four months at another as a participant-observer. She identified five female skills areas for police work from her interviews with the instructors at these training schools. The areas where women had an advantage were (1) handling female victims, especially of sex offenses, (2) handling children and women (presumably whether victim, perpetrator, or plain citizen), (3) doing female searches, (4) showing more empathy for people in general, and (5) not trying to prove anything (manliness was mentioned) in their interactions with others. Women's greater reliance on the ability to interact with people was linked to *not* learning to rely on aggressiveness.

While a later chapter of this book takes up changes in training and fitness programs linked with the influx of women into the police, here we will simply present the fitness profile of the average woman and average man who enter law enforcement training. And what women can expect over three months of training.

Gregory Kuntz (1985) says the average woman to enter the Federal Law Enforcement Training Center (FLETC) at Glynco, Georgia is 29 years old, 5 foot 5 inches tall, weighs 138 pounds, and can run a mile and a half in 17 minutes. She has more body fat than the typical male (23 percent compared to 16 percent) and, while more flexible in her lower back than men, she can bench press only 60 percent of her body weight compared to men who can bench press 95 percent of their body weight.

She may enter FLETC with a lower level of fitness, especially in upper body strength and cardiovascular endurance, but her percentage improvement is usually greater than that of males, says Carolyn Diskin (1985). Women are 20 percent of the total student population at FLETC and those numbers are important. Women often use the company of other women for support and assistance as they establish and maintain a regular exercise regimen. Once women become habitual exercisers, their self-confidence and personal image are stronger, and a support group is no longer so important. Diskin also commented that the majority of male students have reacted very positively to having women in the traditional male province of weight room and gymnasium.

Diskin says women who participate in regular weight training show a 34 percent improvement in upper body strength and can bench press over 80 percent of their body weight. Mandatory training also improves cardiovascular endurance by 23 percent, with mile and one half running times dropping to about 13 minutes. And body fat is also reduced from 23 percent to 19 percent, an 18 percent improvement.

The idea behind FLETC's Physical Efficiency Battery, that is, the five tests given before and after training at the Center, is not only to identify individuals who might have significant health risks, but to motivate officers to maintain a regular fitness program throughout their career. Women are more motivated by the desire to lose weight and fat and to firm leg and thigh areas. Men are more motivated to improve their upper body strength and athletic performance. By setting the 70th percentile for one's sex and age as everyone's goal, women who have been less athletic and sports-oriented than men have a realistic chance of attaining their personal goals. For women jocks there are certificates of excellence, for marginal women, just improving ten percent by the end of the program is acceptable.

THE QUESTION OF STYLE

"Women make good police concludes ex-Chicago cop" is the title of a squib in the March 1981 issue of *Police Chief.* This particular ex-cop, after spending 560 hours riding along with women officers in Cook County, Illinois, said women especially excelled at interviewing crime victims. He felt women's lack of physical strength was more than compensated for by carrying batons and firearms, and by the tendency of men to meekly submit to arrest when confronted by a woman officer. These observations, by no means unique, contribute to the literature on style of policing. How an officer *behaves* as he or she performs the job—that's what is meant by style.

The style of women police up to the 1960s was informal, sympathetic, protective rather than punitive, the style of the social worker in the field. In contrast, the style of the policeman was the man in control whose style reflected the macho stereotypes of aggression, dominance, force, and physical prowess. And a natural holdover from this segregated past is the persistence of stereotyped beliefs such as men aren't sensitive and gentle enough to deal with women and children, and women aren't aggressive enough to handle adult males.

But what about today? Now that women are on patrol in numbers, are the old stereotypes observed in actual behavior? Now that officers of both sexes have more flexibility in style, how do women behave compared to men? And men compared to women? Given the freedom to get the job done with any style that is effective, do the sexes still have distinctive ways of behaving?

As I indicated earlier in this chapter, research on styles is sparse. We have only Martin's and Wexler's observational studies to refer to.

The Style of the POLICEwoman versus the policeWOMAN

The heart of Susan Martin's (1980) doctoral dissertation, the book *Breaking and Entering,* is a chapter devoted to policing styles (pp. 185–203). Martin identified in the 28 women officers she got to know in Washington, DC in 1975–76, two polarized styles, the POLICEwoman style and the policeWOMAN style. It is important to stress that she said that *most* women fell somewhere in between these two extremes. There are not two distinct, widely separated groups of women.

What Martin says is behind these two styles is that these women (and women who enter any male-dominated occupation) must chose to be either deprofessionalized or defeminized. That is, male norms dictate that either a woman coworker remains a lady, a junior partner, the weaker sex, who performs traditional woman's roles and tasks within the occupation (deprofessionalization), or she becomes a strong law enforcement officer, a professional who tries to do the job like any other male officer, and a competitor who tries harder and overachieves (p. 186).

The POLICEwoman's style is to be tough, assertive, independent, loyal to the organization, ambitious, and eager for promotion. The policeWOMAN's style is to be ladylike, service-oriented, unassertive, passive on patrol, and yearning for a nonpatrol assignment but not promotion. POLICEwomen want to be accepted as professionals; police-WOMEN want to be accepted personally, and treated as ladies.

Martin presents a poignant picture of the most disadvantaged woman when it comes to adapting to patrol, the young black woman from a working class family. There are advantages to having come from a *very deprived* background, and advantages to being middle-class, white, older, and more experienced. But a young woman from a poor but respectable home has been raised to be a little lady. She is, therefore, more shy, unassertive, uncomfortable, hesitant, and timid on patrol than women from other backgrounds. Her's is the style of the policeWOMAN. Martin says that to ignore differences in self-confidence and assertiveness among rookies and not give people who need it special training only perpetuates their difficulties (p. 131).

Judie Wexler (1985) has written about styles as well. She distinguishes two kinds, the highly specific styles women police use to relate to men officers. And a general style, the total way a woman goes about the job of police officer, which women either had or did not have. This latter general style is not unlike Martin's global POLICEwoman style. Wexler studied 25 women officers, most of whom like Martin's sample, were in between these two extremes of professionalism.

In terms of how they related to men officers, the women had three styles: neutral-impersonal, semimasculine, and feminine. (The three styles are also discussed in the chapter on stress.)

There was no hint in Wexler's article that any of her California women were as deprofessionalized as some of Martin's Washington, D.C. police WOMEN. Wexler's more professional women, however, used the neutral-impersonal style with the men, while the less professional women used the semimasculine or feminine styles in interacting with the men. Semimasculine and feminine style women saw nothing condescending about letting men help them or tease them, but they sacrificed a good work reputation in the bargain.

What seemed to come first for the masculine and feminine style women was their relationship to the men, and from it came their general style of doing the job. In contrast, the neutral-impersonal style women *got this style of relating to men officers from a deeper, professional style of doing the job.*

Neutral-impersonal style women believed women did certain aspects of police work differently than men. They had developed special techniques which they thought were just as effective, and sometimes better, than men's techniques. These new techniques defined a different, woman's style of policing. It is a style that does not rely foremost on physical strength and it is a style that uses femaleness, when appropriate, to do a better job. These professionally-oriented women trusted that, in the long run, their techniques would prove that women can do just as good police work as men.

In contrast, the women who related to the men with a semimasculine style emphasized going along with the program and did not expect to change the men in any substantial way. They, the feminine, and mixed style women changed their work behaviors so that they would not be a threat to the men. They were rewarded by receiving less stress from the men than neutral-impersonal style women who were challenging the masculine, physical style of policing with a new professional style.

A big issue here, obviously, is the whole question of desirable behavior, effective behavior. What are the standards against which every officer's performance should be judged? Is a given behavior passive and ineffective or passive and effective? Is another behavior aggressive and ineffective or aggressive and effective? The most important thing is not whether a behavior is passive or aggressive, but whether it is effective or not.

Does women's lesser use of strength and aggression work equally effectively? In specific situations as well as in general? Are women being rated fairly when they do the job differently than men, or punished or rewarded for doing it differently? These are style issues begging for investigation.

Women Working Together

Until childhood sexual stereotyping becomes less pronounced and more assertive female police candidates start showing up, what can departments do to counteract women's learned passivity, asked Linn and Price (1985, p. 76). Assign women instructors to the academy and field training. Assign women new to patrol to more experienced women partners who can provide physical training to improve the novices' ability and confidence. Women working together creates peer pressure to combat passivity and provides role models to inspire self-confidence and the confidence of male colleagues.

Susan Martin (1980, p. 125 and 130) quotes from two interviews to support this idea that women police have a lot to gain from working together. If a woman has a woman supervisor, she is less likely to cry and ask for a different assignment. Even though she may be scared, she goes out and proves to herself that she can do it. If a woman has a woman partner, they share the work equally. Working with other women, a woman officer learns to trust her judgment and use her authority faster than when working with men.

Martin noted that women officers who had initially done undercover work went on to subsequent patrol activities with great knowledge and self-confidence. Undercover work had forced them to develop initiative and independence. They had the same self-reliance and decision-making capacity that twenty-three women gained in the summer of 1974 when the department assigned them to plainclothes detail to do a crackdown on prostitution. These women, *working together,* discovered they could defend themselves and make arrests on their own. Their self-confidence and maturity increased palpably as the undercover detail extended in time. A great spinoff was how impressed male officers were with the women's strengths, even to trusting them as partners in the future (p. 132).

Because of the serendipitous effects of this special prostitution detail, Martin recommended that women on patrol be assigned together regularly, rather than departments discouraging female partnerships. Many women police act more independently and assertively when working with a female partner than a male partner. Similarly, using women as training officers, particularly for female rookies, provides the kind of role models male rookies have had all along (p. 212).

There is an unforgettable anecdote in Bryna Taubman's *Lady Cop* (1987, p. 196) on this theme. Three patrol cars in New York City converged on a van loaded with VCRs, TVs, radios, and three males armed with knives and wanted for robbery. The van was pulled over and while three officers guarded the men, guns drawn, the other three officers pushed them up against the van, kicked their legs apart, and searched them. Then two more radio cars arrived with a sergeant who smiled and laughed and taunted the men for letting a bunch of women catch them. Each of the three cars contained two women partners and it must have been a wonderful sight!

One of the most interesting aspects to Molly Martin's (1988) interview with Rose Melendez, San Francisco Police Department, is that Rose had been a partner for several years with Pam Wermes from the same academy class. When the two women first approached their lieutenant and said they wanted to work together, he laughed, and gave them a car in a very rough area where the felonies were homocides, knifings, shootings, and bank robberies. They went on to make "fantastic arrests," and because their training had been so grueling, they could lay out anybody who challenged them "in a matter of seconds."

SUMMING UP

Catherine Jones (1987a, 1987b) has given us data demonstrating once again that women are as competent at patrol as men. Women's strengths lie in such socialized traits as empathy and less aggression in interacting with others. Women's limitations, in the realm of physical agility and strength, can be significantly affected by exercise programs aimed at cardiovascular endurance.

If women police have a different style than men police, women police have different styles among themselves. Some behave in a semimasculine fashion, others use their femininity to advantage. However, the style which promises to leave its imprint upon the police is the style of the POLICEwoman. She wants to be accepted as a professional more than anything else. She has endured more stress from men because of her assertiveness and ambition. But the fact that she believes women have unique and equally effective techniques for policing will ultimately create a better police service.

Chapter 9

PERCEPTIONS OF PERFORMANCE

As I said in the preface, the literature of the 1980s seems to focus on what everyone thinks of the performance of women police. In contrast, the 1970s evaluation studies focused more on objective indices of that performance, such as arrests made, complaints received, scores earned, and incidents handled.

After realizing there was this current concern about differing *perceptions* of women's performance, I tried in this chapter and the one preceding it, "Performance and Style of Policing," to separate perceptions from actual performance. Hence, in the previous chapter, I emphasized objective and physical measures of performance, while here I emphasize attitudes and opinions about performance. Chapter 8, ideally, would have been solely about studies of women's performance and behavior measured by unbiased, reliable, cut-and-dried counts, test scores, records and logs, except that few people are doing that kind of evaluative research anymore.

The truth is, of course, that subjective and objective measures overlap. When a sergeant *rates* an officer's performance on a 5-point scale, there is bound to be some *subjectivity* in that rating. When a citizen says that she perceives women better at handling rape victims than men, and not as good at handling robberies, there is some *objectivity* to her perception.

In any case, this chapter is about what people *think* about women officers' performance, a subject of interest to 1980s' researchers. I will start with a typical study of perceptions that, however typical, does not fit neatly anywhere else in the chapter!

Ernie Hernandez (1982) looked into how 128 male deputy sheriffs felt about four photographs he showed them together with one of two biographical descriptions. The pictures varied the "femininity" of four women police officers essentially by the uniform they wore. A skirt, nylons, high heels, and purse, on the one hand, and, on the other hand, deputy's slacks, boots, and gun in holster on hip. Their hair was also "pretty and girl-like" versus pulled back or cut short. The biographical sketches that accompanied these "masculine" or "feminine" pictures described a very competent woman or an incompetent woman who needed improvement. How would the men rate the four combinations of photograph and biography—feminine/incompetent, feminine/competent, masculine/incompetent, masculine/competent, on three scales: likeability, acceptability as a patrol partner, and acceptability as a staff employee?

No doubt about it. These men wanted competence. My reading of Hernandez' data is that these men liked and were personally attracted to women who were both feminine and competent, but when it came to a patrol partner or someone in a staff position, they wanted competence and didn't care how feminine-appearing a woman was. Competence was more important both to being liked personally by the men and accepted as a colleague rather than having a "feminine" hairdo, lipstick, jewelry, and a skirted uniform.

Whose perceptions, then, have researchers been interested in? Male officers, certainly, as Hernandez was, and also female officers. Then citizens, male and female. We will begin with the citizens.

CITIZEN PERCEPTIONS OF
WOMEN OFFICERS' PERFORMANCE

Throughout the evaluation reports of the 1970s, there were allusions to women's ability to "defuse potentially violent situations," their "pacifying quality" and "calming effect." Horne (1980, p. 112) relates this nonaggressive behavior not only to women's socialization, but to society's expectations that women will be less hostile and less physical than men.

Susan Martin (1980) devoted Chapter 7 (pp. 158–182) in *Breaking and Entering* to police-citizen interaction. She contends that the best officers, of both sexes, not only use their occupational status of police officer to interact effectively with citizens, but that they are flexible enough to use other "irrelevant" statuses, one of which is their sex (p. 163).

What does this mean for women officers? It means bringing to policing a style of interaction that often includes smiling more than men officers, greater politeness in making requests, greater willingness to listen, and more compassion. Martin says it takes women longer to learn how to put on an "I-mean-business" face and longer to learn the posture, carriage, and mannerisms which convey "I am a strong, authoritative police officer." But when women have mastered these assertive, "masculine" stances, they have a wider range of communication than men because they can also use their "feminine" nonthreatening behaviors. It's OK for a woman to play the stern mother chastising a wayward child. It's OK for a woman to appeal to a man's masculinity to get him to exercise self-control. It's OK for a woman to hold an injured or dying person in her arms. These are ways women use their sex status to advantage, to be effective police officers (pp. 174–175).

One of the advantages advanced by women's supporters to having more women in the police is that women's greater tact and helpfulness and lack of aggressiveness will improve relations with the community. Women are also said to come to the job with greater prior experience working with people and greater identification with citizens' needs and complaints.

Are citizens more satisfied with women police than men police?

Kennedy and Homant's (1983) study of 90 abused women living in shelters concluded that the 34 percent who had contact with women police had a more favorable opinion of women officers than the rest of the group who had had contact only with men police. Interviews revealed that what the women appreciated most about women officers was their ability to show concern and supply practical information.

Forty percent of the ninety women said that in the future they wanted two men to come to their aid, 8 percent wanted two women, and 52 percent preferred a male and a female officer. Sixty percent of the entire group wanted at least one woman officer present.

These abused women said women officers were more likely to understand a woman's side of the problem and men police were more understanding of the man's side. They also felt men officers were more likely to calm a man down, as well as prevent violence or injury, and to arrest a man. Men and women officers were perceived as equally likely to listen to problems and give helpful advice. Overall, the picture of perceived abilities of men and women police gave women the edge *only* in understanding the woman's point of view.

However, when the group with contact with women police was compared to the group with no contact, the Contact group rated the overall police response as significantly more helpful than the No Contact group. Further, the Contact group rated women police's ability to perform various tasks as significantly greater than the No Contact group. In particular, 70 percent of the Contact group said women officers could calm men down versus only 38 percent of the No Contact group.

A study with results contrasting to Kennedy and Homant used data from the late 1970s. Steel and Lovrich (1987) found that the citizens of cities with a greater percentage of women officers had no greater confidence in the police than cities with a smaller percentage of women police.

They used public opinion data collected in a survey sponsored by the Law Enforcement Assistance Administration (LEAA) in 1977. This LEAA survey was done in 160 cities and involved over 1,000 citizens. Steel and Lovrich knew from a 1978 survey they had done what the percentage of women officers was in each of 250 American cities. This enabled them to give 562 of the 1,000 LEAA citizens a "women police officer utilization score" for the particular city they lived in.

Steel and Lovrich then divided these 562 citizens into two groups, those who were served by police departments that employed 2 percent or less women, and those that employed between 3–14 percent. Then they looked at how the two groups had responded to a LEAA survey item having to do with confidence in one's local police department. The two groups proved to be equally confident.

Steel and Lovrich's study is more provocative and stimulating than conclusive. For one thing they did a secondary analysis. They used someone else's data rather than design a study for their own fresh sample of citizens. How would their results have differed if they had gathered their own data? How would it have changed things to measure confidence in the police with a more reliable instrument containing several items rather than a single item? How might findings have changed if done in 1987 when there was a better range of percentage of women than 0–14 percent? And inasmuch as Steel and Lovrich's 562 participants lived in over 80 different cities, might conclusions be firmer if based on a greater number of participants in fewer cities?

Differences Between Women and Men Citizens' Perceptions

Do women and men citizens differ in attitudes toward women police? Offhand, we'd certainly think so. We'd expect women to be more prowomen, given what we know about the negative attitudes of male officers toward women officers.

In his 1983 article on the impact of women officers on community attitudes toward police, Homant reviewed the results of two mail surveys sent out in the Detroit area three months apart in time.

The first survey found the Detroit metropolitan area fairly evenly split on the issue of whether women were capable of being full-fledged police officers. Forty-nine percent of 144 respondents agreed they were, 51 disagreed. The image of the police these people held was as concerned, firm, dedicated, and hard working individuals. Sixty percent of the citizens had a favorable image of all police officers, 30 percent were unfavorable, and ten percent were neutral.

Homant found participants who thought women fully capable of being police officers were more likely to be young, black, female, liberal, and from the city rather than the suburbs. There were also clear ideological differences between those who favored women and those who didn't. Those favoring women were more in favor of women's rights, saw police as too aggressive, and were more in favor of local control of police.

Homant's later survey was sent out as part of an experiment to see if a letter extolling the virtues of women police would change people's attitudes. The letter received in between the surveys contained quotes from Jane Fonda, Joyce Brothers, and Ann Landers to the effect that women police were tactful, diplomatic, good dealing with women, and capable at handling hazardous assignments. The letter was sent to only half of the second survey sample, the idea being to compare its impact on recipients.

Unfortunately, at the same time as the experiment, the Detroit press was focusing on a local incident involving the allegation of cowardice in women police. The letter backfired and only served to remind recipients of this incident. They reacted accordingly. Those who received the letter were *less* likely to see women as capable of being police officers than people who didn't get the letters.

Karin Winnard (1986) did a study of citizen attitudes toward women and men police in Irvine, California. She sent a mail survey to her 259 respondents, of whom 53 percent were men. The survey presented four scenarios and asked respondents if they preferred assistance from a male officer, female officer, or had no preference.

The four scenarios were robbery, burglary, vehicular accident, and rape. Winnard predicted that men would be preferred for the robbery, burglary, and vehicular cases, but women preferred for the rape case. This is exactly what she found. Further, for two of the four scenarios, sex of citizen interacted with preferred sex of officer in this way: Men significantly more often than women wanted a male officer in the case of robbery, and a female officer in the case of rape. In both of these situations the women preferred *either* a male or female officer twice as often as the men.

Winnard speculated that men in general want another male in situations calling for stereotypical male attributes because of the idea that physical strength gives them better protection. They may also want females in situations calling for stereotypical female skills because they, as males, might not feel adequate in meet a victim's immediate needs. But perhaps Winnard got the results she did because Irvine women have less traditional values than Irvine men, or had had more contacts with female officers than Irvine men, but Winnard had no way of testing these two ideas.

Koenig and Juni (1981) explored antiwomen police sentiment in a sample of 569 citizens, 233 men and 336 women, most of them students on college campuses in New York State.

They used three kinds of antiwomen measures. One was a *general antiwomen attitude scale* with items about women's supervisory abilities, women's liberation, women's interest in family versus career, women's ability to handle stress and the like. The second measure had eleven complex items in which participants recommended disciplinary action to hypothetical stories about a police officer's misconduct. There were clearly harsh and clearly mild choices to be made, for example, between "transfer to desk duty" versus "no action." The authors thought of this as a subtle, *covert measure of discrimination against women police* since it allowed them to compare just how punishing respondents would be to male and female officers.

The third measure was a *antiwomen police attitude scale.* This scale had 12 items tapping how competent women police were thought to be and whether respondents recommended there be fewer women police, no change, or more women police.

Koenig and Juni found that the average scores of their male and female respondents on all three attitude measures differed significantly. Women had far more positive attitudes toward women in general and toward women police on both the obvious and the subtle instruments.

I think some of the details of the *antiwomen police attitude scale* are worth relating because, while the men respondents were not as prowomen as the women respondents, nonetheless they revealed a lot of support for women police. True, 87 percent of the women agreed that women police are as competent as men police, but 66 percent of the men agreed as well. Likewise, 87 percent of the women thought women should do detective work, but 67 percent of the men said so too. And while 76 percent of the women agreed that a woman officer is as good a partner for a man as another man, 51 percent of the men also agreed.

Should policewomen get foot patrol duties? Yes said 79 percent of the women and 61 percent of the men. Should policewomen be inspectors and police chiefs? Yes said 89 percent of the women and 82 percent of the men. Do policewomen suffer more injuries than policemen? Are policewomen absent more than policemen? To both these items 90 percent of the women disagreed and 86 percent of the men also disagreed.

And, in spite of women participants being more lenient to women officers overall, they actually differed from men participants in their reactions to only four of the eleven stories. Women respondents' punishment of women officers was harsher when the female officer had refused to have a female partner because of her alleged incompetence, and harsher if the women officer had been in a car accident in which a civilian was killed. In contrast, women respondents were more lenient to women officers if a hostage was killed in a rescue attempt, and when a woman officer had wounded an innocent suspect.

Consider this: Only 12 percent of the male respondents and 4 percent of the female respondents said there should be fewer women police. Also 50 percent of male respondents and 84 percent of female respondents said women police were as effective *or more* effective than men police. What Koenig and Juni have demonstrated is that citizen support for women police is growing, at least among the younger, better educated, middle class populace, and growing, as we might expect, faster among the female half of that population.

WOMEN AND MEN OFFICERS'
PERCEPTIONS OF WOMEN'S PERFORMANCE

Bloch, Anderson, and Gervais (1973) included an extremely interesting study of perceptions of women's behavior in their classic evaluation research in Washington, DC. Their results are presented as a list of twelve personality traits useful to a patrol officer, rated from most important to least important by police officials. The traits are followed by the percentages of officials, men officers, and women officers who rated women either "as likely or more likely" as men to have those traits.

There was only one trait for which women officers gave a percentage less than 50 percent—the trait "strong" (43 percent). Here in descending order are the traits for patrol the women felt they had *as much or more of than men* (their percentages in parentheses): decisive (91), persuasive (87), intelligent (84), understanding and compassionate (84), observant (82), calm and cool (78), leader (75), command respect (75), aggressive (68), courageous (66), emotionally stable (63), and strong (43).

These figures demonstrate that despite officials' and male officers' negative opinions, the women maintained a positive opinion of themselves. What would this same study find today? Can we get some idea from the studies which have been done since then, how women currently might rate themselves on the twelve traits?

Janus, Janus, Lord, and Power's (1988) survey of women officers included several items about the women's perceptions of others' perceptions of their performance. For example, 69 percent of these women perceived that the public was just as supportive of them as they were of the men, and 15 percent thought the public was more supportive (and 13 percent thought the public was less supportive). Similarly, 78 percent believed the public had confidence in their performance, 19 percent were unsure, and only 3 percent perceived that the public had no confidence in them.

As for their supervisors, they believed that if they had a problem on the job stemming from being a woman, the supervisor's response would be "excellent" for 27 percent, and "satisfactory" for 44 percent. Twenty-nine percent didn't know or felt their supervisor would not be supportive. Another indication of supervisors' positive perceptions was that only 29 percent thought calls were screened before dispatch so that the women wouldn't get "hot" calls.

How accepting of women police were male colleagues? Only 8 percent said "completely," but 62 percent said "mostly," and 30 percent perceived it was with "some difficulty." How much confidence did male colleagues have in their performance? Again, only a very small percentage felt it was complete, 12 percent, with 53 percent saying "mostly," and 35 percent crediting the men with "some confidence."

The Bloch, Anderson, and Gervais (1973) study also gives us an idea of what these new women felt their skills would be like after a year's experience on the street. Here are 13 skills and the percentages of the women who felt women's skill level would be satisfactory: writing reports, 91 percent; cruising around and observing, 90 percent; questioning rape victims, 88 percent; getting information at crime scenes, 88 percent; handling victims of armed robbery, 88 percent; settling family disputes, 86 percent; handling traffic accidents, 85 percent; handling disorderly females, 73 percent; arresting prostitutes, 68 percent; dispersing noisy juveniles, 66 percent; handling drunks, 64 percent; handling situations where someone has a knife or gun, 63 percent; and, last, handling disorderly males, 52 percent.

These self-perceptions are remarkably like those of U.K. women officers when asked what strengths they thought women possessed. Allison Morris (1987, p. 142) reviewed the findings of P. Southgate reported in a 1981 British *Police Journal* on 680 women police officers' statements about their capability for various tasks and situations compared to male officers. There was only one situation, dealing with a crowd of 4–6 male drunks, in which the majority believed they coped worse than a man.

On the other hand, their strengths compared to men were in "questioning victims of rape/indecency offenses," "child-abuse cases," and "interviewing female suspects." They felt they had the *same* capability as the men at such tasks as general-purpose motor patrol, getting information at crime scenes, observation work, traffic accidents, foot patrol, and domestic disputes. The only other two situations in which a sizeable number (38–39 percent) felt they would do worse than the men was in "threatening situations where someone has a knife or gun," and "interviewing male suspects." Even in these two situations, however, over half of these women constables and sergeants thought their capability to be the same as a man's.

Vega and Silverman (1982) studied 826 women and men officers in the Tampa Bay area of Florida. The men had a median of six years experience, the women two years, in the police service. They filled out a 38-item questionnaire, the focus of which was the effectiveness of women as police officers.

The men and women differed little, or very much, regarding women's patrol abilities depending on the situation. To start with, only 17 percent of the women felt women should *not* be patrol officers versus 48 percent of the men. Further, 60 percent of the women and 16 percent of the men felt women were *as effective* as men on patrol.

As for effectiveness in eleven situations, here are the percentages for the women first, followed by the men, who believe women *are effective:* *crowd control,* 50 percent, 15 percent; *arresting drunks,* 70 percent, 33 percent; *traffic control,* 93 percent, 75 percent; *arresting felons,* 70 percent, 33 percent; *juvenile work,* 97 percent, 90 percent; *undercover,* 97 percent, 90 percent; *arresting a female,* 87 percent, 60 percent; *domestics disturbance,* 77 percent, 45 percent; *dealing with rape victims,* 97 percent, 90 percent; handling *firearms* and other weapons, 86 percent, 42 percent. A big difference between the men and women was the number who thought women as skilled as males in *pursuit driving:* 70 percent of the women, 15 percent of the men.

Participants were also asked if they "wouldn't mind female backup" in four situations. Here are the percentages for the men: *fight in progress,* 12 percent; *robbery in progress,* 31 percent; *burglary in progress,* 40 percent; *domestic,* 48 percent. Regarding the women's responses to these items, Vega and Silverman report that 47 percent felt another female was acceptable backup in a fight, while between 66 and 90 percent of the women wouldn't mind female backup in the robbery, burglary, and domestic situations.

Some other items should be mentioned that have to do with style. Are women *strong* enough for patrol? *Assertive* enough? Too *soft-hearted?* Too *panicky?* Does a woman's presence *calm* a violent subject?

Seventy-five percent of the men thought women weren't *strong* enough, but only 17 percent of women. Fifty-eight percent of the men thought women could not handle violent situations versus 17 percent of the women. Forty-two percent of the men thought women weren't *assertive* enough, but only 3 percent of the women. Twenty-five percent of the men felt women were too *soft-hearted* and too easily *panicked,* versus less than 10 percent of the women. And only 13 percent of the men said a woman's presence calmed a violent subject, whereas 53 percent of the women said it did.

Last, there is the issue of whether or not women were deliberately not assigned to violent areas out of a sense of protectiveness on the part of supervisory personnel. Fifty-two percent of the men thought so, versus "over one-third" of the women.

Vega and Silverman commented that these women police officers had strong positive feelings regarding their emotional preparedness for police work. But the men had their doubts and so did the supervisors the authors interviewed. They wanted to see more assertiveness. Vega and Silverman suggested that if an agency wanted more assertiveness, it should provide assertiveness training for anyone who needed "remediation," male or female. They did not suggest that women adopt a macho image. In fact, they defended women's socialized strengths, such as the calming effect, saying these strengths should be incorporated into more police work.

The calming effect, or relying on verbal techniques and using the fact that suspects are hesitant to fight with a woman, was the basis for sixteen of the 25 women Wexler and Logan (1983) studied saying women officers were less likely than men to get into physical confrontations. Many of these women did not see the job as very dangerous and gave examples of how they used reasoning, nonaggressiveness, and negotiation to control situations and keep from getting hurt.

Seventy-one percent of 191 male state police officers concurred with these women by agreeing with a survey item that women are better than men at calming highly agitated individuals (Weisheit and Mahan, 1988, p. 150). Ninety-three percent of these men thought women were better than men at dealing with people involved in traffic accidents, even though they thought women officers were more likely to panic in tense situations (57 percent agreement).

Following up on Vega and Silverman's work, Love and Singer (1987) had 75 women and 103 men police officers in New Zealand complete a questionnaire that had them rate their own general effectiveness at police work, and specific effectiveness in handling four situations: violent offenders, domestic disputes, riot situations, and youth aid problems. They also rated their psychological well-being and their job involvement. (Their job satisfaction is also discussed in the chapter on job satisfaction.)

There were no differences between the men and women in terms of psychological well-being (it was positive), nor in terms of job involvement (also positive), nor in terms of general effectiveness at police work. As the authors put it, the women, like the men, had confidence in their abilities and effectiveness to carry out their policing duties. But when it came to the four situations, Love and Singer report that while the women's and men's self-ratings did not differ with respect to domestic disputes or youth aid problems, the women rated themselves as less effective in handling violent offenders and riot situations.

Homant and Kennedy have two publications (1984, 1985) which refer to 62 women and 89 men officers in Michigan who gave their perceptions of the behaviors women officers use to deal with domestic violence. The officers filled out a questionnaire that contained an Involvement in Family Fights scale and several background questions. The relationship between Involvement and background is taken up in the chapter on values and attitudes. Here is the appropriate place, however, to deal with perceptions of women police in violent domestic situations.

Referring first to the 1985 article, Homant and Kennedy's questionnaire contained four questions having to do with how female officers handle family fights. One question had simply to do with whether the officer thought women handled family fights differently than men, to which 64 percent of the women and 45 percent of the men agreed. They were invited through an open-ended question to describe just how women were different.

The question of the four that showed the largest sex difference had to do with women having a hard time calming men down. Only 18 percent of the women agreed with this versus 57 percent of the men. Only 14 percent of the women agreed that women automatically side with other women in domestic situations versus 39 percent of the men. Last, 51 percent of the men said that they handled fights differently when their partner was a woman versus 31 percent of women.

Comments were written in by 33 women police and 35 men police. The two groups differed radically in their perceptions. Only two men had anything complimentary to say about women, the majority complaining that women lacked assertiveness.

In contrast, all 33 of the women's comments were favorable toward women. They viewed women police as being more patient, helpful and understanding, and less likely to escalate a conflict.

Is the same behavior being evaluated positively by one group and negatively by the other? Or are the men selectively recalling incidents to fit their stereotypes? Or are the women simply being defensive? Maybe all of the above, say Homant and Kennedy.

Now to Homant and Kennedy's 1984 article which concerns the content of the comments made by the women and men officers who believed the sexes handled family fights differently. What traits lay beneath the women's behaviors?

To answer this question, Homant and Kennedy gave 16 graduate students (eight men and eight women) the comments and a list of 30 adjectives. The students did not know the sex of the authors of the comments. The students' task was to read each comment and the pick out the adjective they felt best summarized that comment. Then Homant and Kennedy looked at the adjectives attached to the male officers' comments and the adjectives attached to the female officers' comments.

The two lists were very different. The men described what Homant and Kennedy call "the helpless cop": weak, passive, uncertain, soft, and slow. The women described what the investigators call "the good cop": helpful, level-headed, professional, concerned, friendly, intelligent, and respectful.

There were four common adjectives to the lists: *professional, feminine, non-violent, and passive.* Both lists, say Homant and Kennedy, seem to agree that women police take a low-key, unassertive approach to domestic violent situations, but that wanting to be helpful is perceived by the men as weakness.

Perceptions from the Academy

Michael Charles (1981) collected two kinds of data on Michigan State trooper recruits. On the one hand, academic records of performance in academic, technical, and physical education. And, on the other hand, peer evaluation forms and questionnaires completed by the recruits themselves.

Here we want to consider what these 50 men and 14 women thought about women as state troopers, their perceptions of the women's job performance in various policing situations, and how the academy experience might have changed their perceptions.

The peer evaluation forms consisted of seven questions about important attributes for troopers to have. Twice during training the recruits filled them out on everyone in their particular small group, the groups consisting of people of the same weight for competitive physical exercises.

On both occasions the women received lower peer ratings than the men, based largely on their physical performance.

The questionnaires, too, were filled out twice, before and after training. The items were a series of specific job situations of three kinds: *physical* situations requiring the use of force; *general* situations calling for judgment; and *technical* tasks such as driving a car. What was the respondent's expectation of women's ability to perform in these situations? This was measured on a five-point scale ranging from "women perform much better than men" to "men perform much better than women."

Both preacademy and postacademy *all* of the men said men were better than women at physical tasks. The women were divided equally on both occasions between thinking men were better and men and women were equal.

As for the general and technical situations, preacademy the men overwhelmingly (85 and 87 percent) felt women were equal to men or better! And the women agreed with these perceptions of equality and female superiority. However, postacademy, while the women stayed the same, the men shifted toward believing in male superiority, even though the male modal response was still equality.

The idea that the academy might change men recruits' original, stereotyped role perceptions of women was sadly mistaken. What happened, instead, was that in the course of training this group of men became very preoccupied with the violent aspects of policing, and convinced themselves that physical power made the difference between life and death.

In contrast, the women came to see the physical side of the job as a very small part of one's overall responsibilities. They knew they were physically weaker than most males, but they also had learned a host of nonphysical tactics to successfully resolve violent situations. The women, unlike the men, simply did not perceive the occupation as a violent enterprise in which physical powers played a significant role. In spite of what turned out to be a hostile learning environment because of the antipathy of a minority of men, the women continued to perceive themselves as physically capable, even if men were stronger than women.

After the academy the women also maintained high self-confidence in their abilities for the general and technical sides of being a trooper. Charles said they did so by perceiving themselves as emotionally and intellectually superior or equal to males after having had the opportunity to compare themselves to the men. They did so because, in fact, they successfuly completed the academy. To accomplish this feat, during training they stayed away from the hostile, antiwomen recruits and associated with men who gave them support and positive feedback.

Diane Pike (1985) gave questionnaires to four recruit classes at Eastern Police Academy and the Midwestern Police Academy. A total of 221 recruits participated, a minority of whom were women. Pike reports that 98 percent of the whole group thought physical skills important in police work. But while 56 percent thought women lacked skills for patrol, only 36 percent said women specifically lacked *physical* skills. Fifty-three percent of these recruits said they would not feel as safe with a female backup, so presumably 47 percent said they did feel as safe with female backup. Indeed, 41 percent of the group said women did not lack any skills for patrol compared to 59 percent who believed men lacked no patrol skills.

Perceptions of Officers-To-Be

Are male police officers-to-be, particularly those getting college degrees in law enforcement, more accepting of women police than current male officers? Kathryn Golden (1981) says yes. She had 134 male law enforcement majors at a midwestern university respond to 15 items having to do with women police. For eight items, "disagree" indicated support of women police, for seven items, "agree" indicated support.

Her results are very hopeful. Fully 85 percent of these men believed women should be given equal opportunity to perform patrol work, and 51 percent agreed women were just as effective as men in the same position. Sixty-four percent wouldn't mind having a woman as patrol partner and among the seniors half believed women had the physical skills and the emotional stability for patrol work.

The men's disagreement with the negative items was equally heartening. Seventy-seven percent did not feel women should be limited to traditional roles in law enforcement; 64 percent did not think patrol was too dangerous for women; sixty percent disagreed that women were too emotional in crises; 56 percent disagreed that women were not aggressive enough for patrol. For all of these items disagreement was stronger the higher the class level of the men.

Golden had two major conclusions. One, men studying for college degrees in law enforcement are more accepting and supportive of women police than the men officers reported on previously. Two, it appears that the university experience is partly responsible for the liberalization of the men's attitudes, inasmuch as they became more receptive to patrolwomen from the freshman to the senior year.

The one survey item about which there was the strongest agreement, which is curious given the personal support the men indicated, had to do with coworker acceptance. Eighty-one percent felt women would have a difficult time with male colleagues. These men, so far, had had no actual agency experience. Yet they apparently knew about the resistance women police traditionally receive from men officers. Will such men continue to hold favorable attitudes toward women police? Or when they become officers, will their attitudes shift towards those of the older men?

Administrative Perceptions of Women's Performance

The 1970s' evaluation study done in Washington, DC found that of all the people who participated in the surveys, officials, especially higher-ups, had the most negative perceptions of women officers. For example, Bloch, Anderson, and Gervais' (1973) list of desirable personality traits for patrol officers gave the percentages of officials, men officers, and women officers who rated women "as likely or more likely" to have these traits than men. The numbers who filled out these surveys were 57 women, 142 men, and 89 officials.

There were twelve traits. The most important to officials were "calm and cool," "decisive," and "observant." The least important were "strong," "courageous," and "leader." The 89 officials were far more negative in their assessment of the women than the men on patrol. These sergeants, captains and lieutenants felt more women than men were "understanding" (7th in importance) and "intelligent" (5th in importance), but that more men than women possessed the other ten traits. Their lowest ratings of the women were for "calm and cool," "aggressive," "strong," and "courageous."

These same officials, when they rated anonymously, perceived new women as far less competent than new men. Captains and lieutenants were more negative than sergeants, saying, for example, that only 30 percent of the women were average or better "general patrol officers" compared to 84 percent of the men, and in "street situations involving violence" only 23 percent of the women were average or better compared to 80 percent of the men.

However, while the sergeants' ratings of the women did not change between 1972 and 1973, to their credit, captains and lieutenants changed their minds. Bloch and Anderson (1974) report that in 1973 these upper-level officials said that "average or above average ability" was observed in 96 percent of the women in handling upset and injured people, in 89 percent in handling domestic fights, in 83 percent in dealing with street violence, and in 83 percent in general competence for patrol.

MEN'S SPOUSES' PERCEPTIONS

A minor concern of researchers in the 1970s was the negative reaction of men officers' wives to their husbands having women officers as patrol partners. Several writers have reported wives were against their husbands working closely with women for fears of romantic entanglements and inadequate backup to the men, for example, Blumberg and Niederhoffer (1985, p. 371), Horne (1980, p. 151), Milton et al. (1974, p. 32), Weisheit and Mahan (1988, p. 148).

On the other hand, Bloch and Anderson (1974) report that Washington, DC officers expected little opposition from their wives if they patrolled with a woman, and the female officers said, too, that their husbands would not care whether they patrolled with a partner of the other sex.

Vega and Silverman's (1982) more recent survey of Tampa area police found that only 36 percent of the men thought their girlfriends or wives would object to a female partner. Men who had attended college and men who had actual experience with women on patrol indicated less objection by their wives.

But we haven't more recent or better data than these on the question of how the spouses of women and men officers feel about partners of the other sex. Perhaps this minor concern has become a miniscule concern.

SUMMARY OF OFFICERS' PERCEPTUAL DIFFERENCES

Looking back over the section above on women and men officers' perceptions of women's performance, how do the sexes compare today in contrast to the findings of the 1970s' Washington, DC evaluation?

Back then the men doubted that the women were their equals, while the women perceived their patrol skills as good as the men's. As a result, the men had a definite preference for patrolling with a male partner, the women only a slight preference for patrolling with a male partner.

Certainly the Charles (1981), Vega and Silverman (1982), and Homant and Kennedy (1984) studies are testimony to continuing sex differences in the perception of women's performance. Women feel strongly that they can do the job of patrol, men continue to doubt it. Pike's (1985) academy data, however, seem to indicate younger officers are getting more comfortable with the idea of backup from women.

Perhaps the women in the Janus et al. (1988) study perceived greater support from supervisors and male colleagues than is there in reality. But if the women are correct, then men's attitudes seem to be shifting somewhat. Men continue to have greatest confidence in women's performance, however, in the more traditional areas of undercover work, traffic control, juvenile work, and working with rape victims.

The most hopeful sign comes from Kathryn Golden's work from which we can see that young officers-to-be wouldn't mind having women as partners and do not think women should be limited to traditional roles in law enforcement.

Chapter 10

RETENTION AND PROMOTION

For two solid years, the men on the third shift would not speak to Ann Roling (Davis, 1982). They resented her as a woman. They resented her as a college graduate. She had a very bad time, she said, very bad. She learned just how vicious police personnel could be, but also learned how human and good they could be. She was able to stick it out because her chief and a couple of other guys *would* talk to her.

She says she is not bitter. She says she picked out what was good and what was bad, what she was going to emulate and what she wasn't. She learned all her lessons the hard way, in the field.

Roling spent eight years moving up the ranks in the University of Missouri Police Department. She became a sergeant at the age of 28, the first woman to ever make that rank in her department. Her police skills were outshone only by her people skills.

At 31, when interviewed, she was the only woman to reach the position of Director of Public Safety for a college (Fredonia State) within the State University of New York (SUNY) system. She was now a police administrator and, while going slow, watching, and waiting, and not changing everything overnight, had plans for installing a group of cadets from the student body into the department. Regular retraining was another of her priorities, as was continuing her nationally recognized work in crime prevention and rape awareness. She got where she was, she said, because she worked so hard for so long, in spite of starting out with very negative experiences.

If the police service cannot retain women, it cannot promote them. If it does not promote them, it will not retain them. But retention comes first. What are the major factors affecting retention of women police officers?

FACTORS AFFECTING RETENTION OF WOMEN

Merry Morash (1986, p. 291) says that despite a hostile workplace environment women police struggle to bring about better working conditions and improvements in the aspects of policing they value the most. However, women officers could bring about change better and faster if they did not suffer from two big impediments: sexual harassment and exclusion from coworker social groups where informal, critical, on-the-job training takes place.

Sexual harassment can be direct and very personal, or it can be impersonal and organizational, such as not providing training suited to women's physiology, uniforms tailored to fit women, or adequate maternity leave. Morash implies that when women police do stay, it is not because of departmental policies on their behalf, but because of their own efforts to make their jobs better.

But departments differ enormously in terms of number of women officers, so some departments are obviously making an genuine effort. Here we want to take up several factors suspected of having an impact upon retention.

Does Type of Management Matter?

The New Jersey State Police all-female police class in 1979 illustrates the difference management commitment to affirmative action can make. In addition to the modifications in the program instituted to get the women as physically fit and willing to use force as men, there were three tactics used with men police as well (Patterson, 1980). First, trainers were told an anecdote about the New York State Police to the effect that when an instructor told his superintendent he couldn't qualify women on the firing range, the superintendent said that if he couldn't do it, he'd find someone who could.

Second, before the women reported for training, the instructors received an in-service program to talk about sexism and were encouraged to vent their feelings on the subject. Third, to prove to the 2,000 male troopers that standards had not been lowered and that the women were getting equally rigorous training, two troopers were brought in every other day to watch the women training. Although some of the women felt mocked by these observers, the superintendent felt many men changed their skeptical minds as a result of their visits.

Even though this experimental, all-woman program was initiated because of a court order, it is clear that the superintendent was solidly behind it and that his support and optimism, sense of being a trail blazer and smasher of "old men's tales," went a long way toward cutting the female dropout rate from 100 percent to 70 percent and actually turning out 30 qualified women troopers (Patterson, 1980).

Another example of management support comes from Texas. As a result of a white woman officer shooting a black man to death after he took her female partner's revolver away, a Dallas councilman suggested a policy of always pairing women with men and blacks with whites ("Dallas police," 1984). But the Chief defended the department's policies which ignored sex and race of patrol teams and said it was an insult to women to suggest they should not be teamed up together. Besides, he said, anyone who suggested that two women couldn't go out on a call together, had not read the Civil Rights Act. The fact was that as the number of women officers continued to rise, the number of women involved in shootings was going to rise as well.

It is probably the case that wherever we find the largest proportions of women in police agencies, we will also find strong management support of women. Management belief in the contribution of women to policing is the cornerstone of successful affirmative action.

Commitment to EEO and Affirmative Action

Potts (1983) recalls the sort of thing that used to happen. A woman who worked in a police dispatch office was summarily dismissed. She claimed sex discrimination. The department defended itself by saying she had not been hired according to the ordinance governing hiring of police officers and therefore she was not entitled to the dismissal procedure for police officers.

However, the court found that she had the appearance and authority of a police officer. She had an ID card saying she had the authority of a police officer. She had a license to carry a concealed pistol. She had a Miranda card and handcuffs. She searched and guarded prisoners and had made an arrest in the station against a person with an outstanding warrant. The court ruled that she had been fired because she was a woman and that she was entitled to the administrative due process police officers were entitled to.

One way departments show commitment to EEO and affirmative action is by no longer denying women equal protection of the law. But what have departments done in a positive way? What commendable actions can be found in the literature that demonstrate that affirmative action is being actively pursued by organizations?

Buzawa's (1984) data collected from 94 officers in Detroit and 76 officers in Oakland illustrate how an active affirmative action program influences officer job satisfaction.

Both cities have police departments with large budgets and high manpower levels, high percentages of minority citizens and people living below the poverty level, and very high crime rates. Yet the determinants of the job satisfaction of their police were quite different, very "situationally determined," to quote Buzawa.

As far as the variable of sex was concerned in predicting job satisfaction, the women in Oakland reported lower job satisfaction than the men, while in Detroit the women were more satisfied than the men. In fact, in Detroit, 62 percent of the men were dissatisfied compared to only 24 percent of the women.

What made the difference? Buzawa says their varying affirmative action programs may be the primary cause. Detroit's program included strong efforts to hire women, so that at the time of the study, 11 percent of the department was female. In contrast, and despite sex discrimination suits, Oakland only had 2 percent women officers. Buzawa's results suggest that affirmative action policies can reverse situations in which women police are more dissatisfied with their jobs than men officers because of isolation, being treated differently, and being underutilized.

One way an organization demonstrates its commitment to equal employment opportunity is by having a clear policy and procedure for handling sexual harassment. Jeffrey Higginbotham (1988), in the Legal Counsel Division of the FBI Academy, says first, such a policy must identify conduct which constitutes sexual harassment. Most intelligent people can define what an "unwelcome sexual advance" and a "request for a sexual favor" consist of, but where intelligent women and men may disagree is conduct that "creates an intimidating, hostile, or offensive working environment" or which has the "effect of unreasonably interfering with an individual's work performance."

The latter is just as much sexual harassment as being asked to submit to a sexual act as a condition of employment. It consists of comments and actions of the employer, supervisors, or coworkers which create an unwelcome work environment based on an employee's sex. Getting the *definition* of sexual harassment across may require a training program so that all employees have a common understanding of what it entails.

Second, says Higginbothom, the policy and procedure must prohibit the offensive conduct and provide for appropriate remedial and punitive measures which are taken if the policy is violated. A mandatory and accessible grievance procedure must exist so that management can move quickly to resolve grievances. Multiple persons must be authorized to receive harassment complaints, and they should include persons of both sexes as counselors.

Third, the policy and procedure must have a mechanism for timely investigation of complaints and all allegations should be treated seriously. Fourth, each instance of sexual harassment must be effectively resolved. Simply having a policy and procedure do not protect an employer from liability; the procedure has got to resolve problems effectively.

Here are two examples to illustrate the problem of defining what is and is not sexual harassment. Higginbotham said it *was* sexual harassment when a woman chronicled eleven events including (1) superiors who refused to acknowledge or speak to her, (2) obscene pictures posted in the station with her name on them, (3) false misconduct claims lodged against her, (4) work schedules manipulated to prevent her from being senior officer on duty thus denying her command status, (5) members of her family being arrested, threatened, and harassed, (6) her office mail and squad car interfered with by other officers, and (7) attempts to implicate her in an illegal drug transaction.

On the other hand, having a male officer place a flashlight between a woman officer's legs from behind *was not* sexual harassment. The judgment was that this was "nothing more than horseplay" and a way to relieve stress in a high-pressure job.

The important thing to remember is that no economic or tangible job detriment has to be suffered to constitute sexual harassment. One of the conditions of any employment is *the psychological well-being of employees.* Thus, when one's psychological well-being is seriously adversely affected by one's working environment based solely on sex, it meets the definition.

Effect of Proportion of Women in the Agency

One of the most depressing accounts of women's "integration" into the police has been written by Patricia Remmington (1983) who chronicled what the Atlanta Police Department was like in the mid-1970s when 10 percent of the department was female. Ten percent may seem like a lot, but on a given shift in a given precinct, there would be only one or two women out of 20 or more officers.

The women weren't allowed to take control of any situation, even directing traffic while a light was being repaired. Everyone preferred a male partner. On every violent call during the year Remmington "rode along," a male officer was present and assumed responsibility. The men did everything they could to remind the women that they were not bona fide members of the group. The men said the women's lack of physical strength and aggressive, authoritative image were why they could not accept them.

The women officers appeared to Remmington to have a different yet effective style of policing, for example, using verbal strategies rather than physical force to get drunks into the police car. The women's style was calming, more peaceful, less physical, but Remmington concluded, until male officers refrained from dominating women officers, this "female style" would never be noticed.

As a byproduct of their token, marginal position, the women did not confront the men with their resentment and frustration. They didn't even tell the men how infuriating continuous sexual teasing and bantering were. Instead, the women took on the men's conservative and cynical attitudes and negative feelings toward citizens. A number of the women had been divorced since becoming officers and felt their jobs had caused their marriages to break up. It seems truly ironic, reading Remmington, that these women had *not* been assimilated into this police department, yet they had changed to be more like the men, emulating the men's attitudes and behavior, and behaving on the job like secretarial assistants rather than real police officers.

The reason for discussing Remmington here, however, is because she stressed one of the implications of her findings was that *numerical equivalency*—no more tokenism—was the solution. Equal numbers of women and men in the police service could change the public's old image of the police as physically powerful, she said, which would in turn let women officers change their male counterparts' attitudes and behavior, rather than the other way around. In the meantime she called for rigorous supervision of backup by the police administration so that women could handle more calls alone. From this the women's self-image would improve and the men's belief in their competency increase.

An Exemplary Study of Tokenism from Holland

Marlies Ott (1989) interviewed 150 members of the Dutch police to study women's tokenism. The 150 interviewees consisted of 3 people from each of 50 police patrol teams which are composed of 15 members. The three people were one woman officer, one man officer, and the sergeant. (All but one of the 50 sergeants were men.) Twenty-four of the 50 teams were "O" teams, meaning that the woman was the Only woman on the team of 15. Twenty-six of the teams were "F" teams, meaning that the woman was one of a Few women on the team. The average percentage of women on the "O" teams was 6 percent; the average of women on the "F" teams was 26 percent. The sergeants' average age was 36, the 100 officers' average age 23.

Ott's two hypotheses were that (1) O women officers would experience disadvantages because of tokenism compared to F women officers, and (2) F men officers would oppose increases in the number of women more than O men officers, because the number of women was reaching a critical mass of 20–40 percent and beginning to threaten the status of the majority.

There were two areas of disadvantage where the O and F women did not differ: *stress* and *absenteeism.* There were no differences in the scores of the two groups on a stress index measuring how often they felt nervous, unsure, lonely, or irritated at work. And no differences between O and F women in the numbers who admitted calling in sick because they were tired of their colleagues.

Did O women feel more *visible,* more paid attention to than their male colleagues were, compared to F women? Yes, 78 percent of them said, versus 32 percent of F women; also 71 percent of O women versus 13 percent of F women felt the sergeant paid extra attention to them, and it was not a pleasant "visibility." They lacked privacy, were looked upon with skepticism, and none of them said they enjoyed it.

Did O women have fewer *informal contacts* than F women? Yes, they did, and they attended parties significantly less frequently because they were made the target of jokes and had to answer unpleasant questions about their lives.

Did O women experience greater *sex-role stereotyping* from supervisors than F women? Yes, the sergeants of O women more often doubted whether the women could do all police tasks and whether a man and a woman working together could handle all calls. The sergeants of F women had fewer doubts about the women, their only concern being whether two women working together could do all beats and shifts. A very strong indication of sex stereotyping of O women was that 60 percent of them had to perform informal "female" tasks such as buying presents for colleagues, making coffee, and tidying up. This was true of just 15 percent of the F women. (But Ott says all this means is that these "female activities" were distributed over more F women.)

Were O women less *accepted* than F women? Yes, 42 percent of O women felt they were the black sheep of the team versus only 11 percent of F women. Ott comments that they did not seem overly bothered by this, or at least indicated that they could understand it.

Were O women subjected to more *sexual harassment* than F women? Yes, although 90 percent of *all* the women said coarse and indecent remarks were made, the F women often said this did not occur on their teams, but elsewhere in the police agency. Sixty-nine percent of all the women also said sex films were shown at work. None of the O women had tried to stop the showing of the sex films, but 19 percent of the F women had tried.

Last, although O women and F women were involved equally in *love affairs* with colleagues, 46 percent of O women had problems with gossip versus only 15 percent of F women.

As for Ott's second hypothesis, regarding the greater resistance of F men over O men, most F men (57 percent) preferred that a man be hired in the event of a job opening, while most O men (63 percent) had no preference. Most F men (75 percent) wanted to keep the number of women in the organization as it was, while most O men (81 percent) wanted more women.

Ott comments that her study did not find any support for the suggestion that two token women on a team become rivals. In teams with two women, they supported each other and got along well, just as did women in teams that had three or four women.

While this is just one study, and more needs to be done on this crucial point, it appears that the tokenism experienced by a lower status entrant into a group (such as women entering a male-dominated occupation) is a negative experience for the token. It also appears that the disadvantages experienced by lower status tokens disappear as their numbers increase.

SHOWING SENSITIVITY TO FAMILY RESPONSIBILITIES

Will more women be retained when the police service accepts some responsibility for the welfare of families of employees?

Pregnancy Leave and Light Duty

The Pregnancy Discrimination Act of 1978 prohibited discrimination on the basis of pregnancy, childbirth, or related medical conditions and required that employers treat these conditions as any other temporary disability with regard to providing employment benefits. So much for the law. How is it being translated into action?

Barbara Hauptman (1989), of the Omaha, Nebraska police, received responses from seven police departments to her call in *WomenPolice* to learn more about other agencies' "maternity leave" benefits. Here is what the Women's Committee of her Police Union submitted, unsuccessfully, as a leave package for negotiation in 1989.

Provision for Family Leave of 80 hours of paid family leave during any 24 month period for any employee for the birth or adoption of a child or to care for the employee's spouse, parent, or child who had a serious health problem (excluding mothers using the birthing leave with pay).

Provision for Birthing Leave of Absence with Pay for women, not to exceed 320 hours in a 24 month period. It was separate from any accrued annual or sick leave and could be taken before and/or after delivery of the child.

Provision for Child Care paid by the city at a facility certified by the state and open 24 hours a day.

Currently, pregnant women working for the Omaha Police may use up their sick and annual leave or take leave of absence without pay when unable to perform normal work duties, as supported by a physician's certificate.

What progress on the maternity leave front did the other departments reveal? The Defiance, Ohio Police Department grants pregnant employees leaves of absence without pay. A physician's certificate is necessary stating that the employee is unable to perform the substantial and material duties of her position. Supervisors can request that employees begin sick leave, vacation leave, or maternity leave at an earlier date than that selected by the employee, but the employee can appeal that action and continue working until a decision is made.

The Detroit, Michigan Police Department takes pregnant women off patrol duties and places them on limited duty status. As far as leave is concerned, women must use up their sick and annual leave and then are placed on Leave Without Pay.

The Nebraska State Patrol considers pregnancy, post-natal recovery, and miscarriage as temporary disabilities. Employees can use sick leave when they are unable to perform duties because of sickness, disability or injury or when their immediate family is ill. Beginning in the fifth month of pregnancy women are placed on special work assignments until they can't perform "any assigned duties." At that point, they can use up their vacation and sick leave. And/or they can go on an unpaid leave of absence not to exceed one year.

In East Hampton, New York, women police can use their sick leave, personal days, vacation days, and any other accumulated days as days off for maternity leave. The town will also loan women thirty days leave if they have less than 30 days, which they then repay the town upon return. Employees get 21 days sick leave a year and can accumulate it up to 320 days.

The Saanich Police Department, Victoria, British Columbia, grants women up to six months unpaid maternity leave. The Fort Wayne, Indiana Police Department allows pregnant women to work light duty and treats pregnancies as it treats illnesses or injuries, letting women use their paid sick time under doctor's orders. Pregnant women may also take up to one year, presumably unpaid leave, as may all officers with serious illnesses or injuries.

The Phoenix, Arizona Police Department says "maternity leave" is a combination of paid sick leave, other paid leave, and up to 2 months unpaid leave. When a pregnant woman's duties are injurious to her health, other temporary assignments will be sought, but if unavailable, she must go on maternity leave.

Hauptman's report also includes the policy of the U.S. Army National Guard and Army Reserve as of 1980. Pregnant soldiers get, presumably paid, 4 weeks of prenatal leave, followed by 6 weeks of postnatal leave.

It was interesting to note that Defiance, Ohio and Phoenix, Arizona provided 30–31 days a year of paid leave of absence for "ordered training" or Military Leave, and Omaha, Nebraska provided 15 paid days a year of Military Leave.

Flexible Schedules and Child Care

Judging from the survey of Garrison, Grant, and McCormick (1988) of 180 members of the International Association of Women Police, unless women have small children, they have no particular shift preference. Only a third of this sample preferred day shift and weekends off. Others clearly liked 4 to midnight and, if assigned to patrol, preferred doing it at night. But when children are involved, it's a different story.

One answer to women's family problems is on-site child care. One of the first such child-care facilities is a pilot program to care for 35 children of NYPD employees right in the monolithic, 15-story One Police Plaza in New York City ("NYPD gears up," 1989). Two-thirds of the 3,200 employees who work there are civilians. Three-quarters of the civilians are women, ten percent of the uniformed officers are women. The child-care center is for both civilians and sworn officers, for both men and women. A lottery system will be used to choose the children who will participate. It will cost $110 a month but subsidies are available.

This NYPD article states that women now make up 12 percent of the NYPD's total uniformed force, representing an increase of 9 percent in the 10-year period since 1978. In order to advertise for the best women, they say, they must be able to offer some really good fringe benefits. And adequate child care for most mothers is right up there.

Women's conflicts about marriage and motherhood, career advancement and career commitment, may be one of the prime motivators for women to leave police work says Mark Pogrebin (1986). He cites studies showing women police have higher divorce rates than men police and lower marriage rates than the national female population. He asks why women police suffer more in their family and social lives than do male officers. It's bad enough that officers' spouses have to put up with insecurity, danger, and antipolice feelings, but women not being accessible to their children because of frequently changing shift assignments and mandatory overtime is very stressful.

Pogrebin calls for greater understanding by police administrators of women police who are also parents. He recommends allowing work schedule modifications on a flexible basis so that women can be with their children when no one else can be. Only if administrators understand women's dual role responsibilities and implement policies that allow them to meet both sets of obligations will the police service retain its women.

Sandra Jones (1986, p. 117) says that while having children may not be the only reason for the loss of U.K. women from policing, it certainly appeared to be the major reason. Only 31 percent of the women she studied were married versus 84 percent of the men. And only 10 percent of the women had children versus 76 percent of the men. Eighty-one percent of men officers and 64 percent of women officers said that most women police left the service because of marriage and the decision to have children. However, men were hostile to the idea of officers getting more regular hours when children were young, and greeted the idea of child care provision with derision.

Even so, organizations must address the issue of family responsibilities or they cannot retain women.

EXPECTATIONS AND DESIRE FOR PROMOTION

We now move to another area of contention for women police, advancement opportunities and promotion realities.

Steinbeck (1985) presents the basic dilemma regarding the promotion of women police. Informal discrimination against women continues. Men consciously and unconsciously deny women camaraderie, verbally harass them, and are reluctant to let them perform assignments as diversified as men get. All of this adversely affects a woman's performance and decreases her opportunities for advancement (not to speak of increasing her feelings of frustration and job dissatisfaction). And the dilemma is that until women hold a higher percentage of administrative and high-ranking positions, they will not be in position to alter discriminatory policies and get rid of harassment.

Nonetheless, numerous sex discrimination barriers to women's promotion have been eliminated across the country by the courts. For example, the Pittsburgh Police Department had a policy of assigning women to Missing Persons with the rank of patrol officer. In order for an officer to be promoted to detective, it was necessary to demonstrate aptitude for investigation, outstanding meritorious service, or unusual bravery. Just how was anybody in Missing Persons going to qualify for promotion? The court ruled that because these women had little opportunity to demonstrate these three traits, the Department was depriving women of equal opportunity for promotion (Potts, 1981).

But just how much do women *want* to be promoted? Do traditional sex-role proscriptions against leadership over men, knowledge of the additional stresses of supervision, and conflicts with family responsibilities conspire to lower women's achievement drive? Do women take the examinations with less frequency? If women are not in the higher ranks, is it because women do not desire to be there? We do not have sufficient information to answer these questions, but here is what we do know.

Evidence that women *do* desire to be promoted was found in Lincoln Fry's (1983) study of 29 women and 261 men who left a county sheriff's department. The women differed from the men in that more of them were in the very lowest rank, were jail custodians, and left for other jobs in law enforcement. When they were interviewed, the women tied it all together by saying lack of promotability was why they left. If they could never get a patrol assignment, they could never be promoted. Fry said the women's desire to compete with men for all departmental assignments, especially patrol, was a reason for the county to come up with "more innovative personnel policies related to the retention of women."

Martin (1980) asked 28 women and 27 men police officers what their five-year aspirations were. Half of both groups wanted promotion or an investigative assignment. Equal proportions of both groups also planned to resign for another occupation (22 percent). The main difference in aspirations of the sexes was that more women wanted "inside" assignments (pp. 70–71). Again, women do desire to be promoted to the same extent that men do.

In Martin's study, however, there were differences in the black and white women's aspirations. Fewer black women desired promotion. More black women wanted to go into areas of policing traditionally reserved for women. The prospects of marriage and childrearing were one of the reasons why the black women were more uncertain about their future in the department. Only one black woman (of 21) predicted she would get promoted or get an inside assignment (p. 72).

Allison Morris (1987) says one of the purposes of P. Southgate's 1981 survey of British women police was to see what effect women's integration in 1975 into mainstream policing had had upon their career aspirations. While 80 percent of men in a comparable sample had applied for promotion, only 50 percent of the women had. A third of the women felt that integration had, in fact, worsened their chances of promotion (p. 143). Still, less than a quarter of the women wanted to go back to the pre-1975 police structure where their prospects of promotion had been better (p. 141).

SUPERVISORY TRAINING

O'Block and Abele (1980) describe the typical process by which women officers today achieve promotion. It is not through lateral entry, that is, being hired directly into specific detective positions, as was the practice prior to the 1960s. Today, instead, it is through the same recruit school and years of patrol duty that men go through, that is, earning a promotion to detective. Once women are detectives, the practice of team policing in specific areas of a city gives women the opportunity to handle the full gamut of investigations rather than being limited to only certain kinds of cases. O'Block and Abele noted the great success of women detectives who have done dangerous nighttime drug undercover work.

And after that success in the field, next comes the exam for sergeant.

Do women aspiring to be sergeants feel as competent as men aspirants? Do the women's training needs for supervision differ from men's training needs? Wexler and Quinn (1985) got 122 men and 21 women patrol officers and inspectors with the San Francisco Police Department to fill out surveys rating their competency on 23 leadership tasks and how much they wanted training on the 23 tasks. Ninety-two percent of this sample took the next promotional exam.

Regarding present competency, for 14 of 23 tasks, the men's self-evaluations of competence were significantly higher than those of the women. There were three types of tasks. *Operational tasks* were routine lead activities such as coordinating searches and advising at the scene of an incident. Examples of *tactical tasks* were familiarity with weaponry and making an assault on an objective. Among *supervisory tasks* were providing training and recommending disciplinary action. The women felt most competent at the latter, the supervisory tasks, and least competent at crisis-situation, tactical tasks.

In contrast to their different self-perceptions of competence, the women and men had very similar priorities regarding training. More than half wanted training on 20 of the 23 tasks. And in general they agreed on which tasks they wanted training in most and least. The one area where the women more strongly wanted training was "commanding personnel at a scene where a sergeant is requested."

But what are the implications of the women's lower self-evaluations of competence at being a sergeant? Wexler and Quinn think they are the result of less patrol experience than the men had, fewer opportunities to successfully take the lead in street situations, and the hostility and nonsupport from men. As far as patrol experience was concerned, 67 percent of the men had 6–10 years compared to only 15 percent of the women.

Wexler and Quinn recommend that training of men and women for sergeant be held together, but that the training experience be shaped through the choice of trainers and materials so that women see themselves as successful leaders and men see the women's competence and accept them as leaders. They also felt the men should work together with the women during training on how to handle the extra challenges women face as new sergeants.

SOME SUPERVISORY EXPERIENCES

Zytowski's (1989) IAWP women demonstrated that women are moving up the ladder. Of the 319 women who indicated what their rank was, 38 percent could be designated as "high level." The 38 percent breaks down to 18 percent corporals and sergeants, 8 percent lieutenants and captains, 8 percent special agents, and 5 percent "master police officers." This last category included not only master police officers, but chiefs of police, U.S. marshalls, sheriffs, and inspectors. In fact, an "other" category of 29 women which could not be easily designated high or low level, included many women involved in training who probably hold rank above a patrol officer or even an investigator/detective, for example, "firearms instructor," "training supervisor," "field training officer," and "law enforcement instructor."

Still, recent, nationwide figures are hard to come by, and we are left at the level of the case study in what we know about women's supervisory experiences.

In 1983, 30 years after becoming a patrol officer, Jayne Thomas Rich was honored by receiving the annual award of the Bronze Shields, a fraternity of black police officers ("Outstanding woman," 1983). Trained as an English teacher and entering the police after losing her job as a security claims analyst, Rich rose through the ranks of the Washington, DC police. She was the first woman to attain a place on the promotional list to captain, earning the highest score on the civil service exam. Lt. Rich retired from the DC service in 1972 and went to Chief of Police positions on three college campuses, Georgetown University, the University of Pennsylvania, and Montclair (NJ) State College.

In August 1988 Rulette Armstead became the first woman and first black to achieve the rank of captain in the San Diego Police Department (Weber, 1989). She was 38 and had been with the police for 14 years. She graduated from college with a degree in sociology and went into police work by accident, just as Rich did. And just like Rich, by applying herself, she advanced from patrol officer to school task force officer to detective, to criminal intelligence sergeant, and executive lieutenant. In 1989 she headed the Communications Division where she supervised 160 people, mostly dispatchers. But she always did more than what her job called for. She was president of the Black Law Enforcement Network, a countywide organization to recruit minorities into the criminal justice system. She was the department's (first) equal employment officer, investigating internal discrimination complaints. And, perhaps most important, given what this chapter is about, she had developed a police sergeants' preparatory course for San Diego City College. She felt there was a need for preparing people better for becoming sergeants, teaching them what they need to know to survive as new supervisors.

Lt. Lucie J. Krause, first and, as of 1982, only woman commander of a vice unit in Cleveland, was described by her chief as very competent, tough but fair, and easy for the men to communicate with (Coyne, 1984). She embodied advice given elsewhere in this chapter. First, she served her dues, spending many years on patrol, including decoy work in prostitution. She continually educated herself, for example, attending the FBI academy's 11-week executive training course, and acquiring in-depth knowledge of state and local vice laws so that she could write departmental guidelines herself. She was democratic, herself working split shifts (early a.m., late p.m.) so that her understaffed 8-person unit could function more effectively. She got good results but wouldn't take the credit alone. She viewed prostitution, for example, as a community problem, for which she went out and got citizen and business support and cooperation. She also maintained the unusual and endearing belief that everyone involved in street prostitution was a victim — legitimate businesses and their patrons harassed by the action, johns who got mugged and robbed in the process, and, yes, the prostitutes, too.

Lt. Julie Smith, Oklahoma City's first woman lieutenant who wanted to be its first woman captain, also served her dues, starting at the age of 22 as one of the first five women patrol recruits in Oklahoma City (Darrow, 1988). She described herself as a small-town girl who married young, had four sons, and had to enter the labor force to support them. She was promoted to sergeant after 11 years, her first six years in undercover operations. Thereafter she was assigned to sex crimes investigations, earning a reputation as one of Oklahoma's foremost authorities on rape. Her style of leading was "like a mother hen with too many chickens." One of the ways she expressed her maternalism was to develop a Felony Apprehension and Surveillance Team (FAST), comprised of young officers who caught criminals in the act of snatching purses or stealing cars. When interviewed she headed the robbery, homicide, and missing persons details and was known for treating her 27 detectives with respect and fairness, because she believed in the competence of her people.

Penny E. Harrington's experience as the police chief of Portland, Oregon, was as negative as Armstead's, Krause's, and Smith's experiences were positive. Harrington blamed criticism of her by the police union and the news media for ending her 17-month tenure as America's sole big-city female chief of the 1980s ("Portland police," 1986).

In spite of the fact that she tried to implement a value-based, participatory style of management and for the first time in over 10 years had weekly staff meetings with the deputy chiefs and captains, she was charged with failing to consult with top commanders. In spite of sending new narcotics officers away to school for special training and creating a new drug unit, she was charged with damaging the department's drug enforcement capability. And, although she created a new juvenile unit aimed at preventing burglaries, she was criticized for not getting the opinions of the people assigned to it.

Harrington instituted a number of policies to open up channels of communication, but she was said to display an "unyielding" management style. And although banning the so-called "sleeper" choke-hold was aimed at being more accountable to Portland's citizenry, the union didn't like it, and Harrington subsequently fired two officers for selling T-shirts labeled "Don't choke 'em; smoke 'em."

Any woman desiring to become a police chief should study Penny Harrington's career carefully. There are many lessons to be learned, much advice to be taken.

WHAT IT TAKES TO BE A LEADER

Two women, a corrections professor and a reserve officer, have summarized what rank and file officers feel are the abilities that go to make a good front-line officer. Masters and Rasmussen's (1983) list of 23 qualities are what police officers told them they wanted to see in colleagues who got promoted to sergeant. Some of the 23 attributes give an edge to men, such as "fraternalness," "self-confidence," and "respect of command and authority." Other attributes are obviously acquired only after joining the service, such as "well-roundedness" defined as varied law enforcement experience, "street experience," "officer effectiveness" defined as not overreacting and not underreacting, and "good officer survival techniques."

But there are also many attributes on this list of leadership qualities where women have a cultural, socialized, learned advantage. For example, (1) "Good listener." (2) "Quiet presence of command" defined as "no obvious machoism; low profile." (3) "Caring, concern, and respect for others," in particular, "taking care of one's staff."

Women's socialization might also give them an edge on these qualities: "straightforwardness and honesty without abrasiveness," "accountability" which includes being willing to admit when you're wrong, and "predictability" which means being punctual and consistent in behavior.

In any case, coming as they did from rank and file men, these attributes reflect a wonderful blend and balance of common sense, stability, and genuineness, that women certainly have at least as much as men do.

A. Vance Stickley in the June and September 1988 issues of *WomenPolice* reports the results of a survey of women chiefs of police. It looks as if there were at least thirty female chiefs in the U.S. in 1987 and Stickley received details about the lives of eleven.

What were these women like? Their time in office was brief, from less than two years to seven and a half years. They were in command in very small departments. The size of the departments ranged from only four to 28 sworn officers and the populations they served numbered from 450 to 35,000 people.

Only three had passed merit exams; for the most part they were political appointees. Nonetheless, all felt it was their experience, education, hard work and perseverance had earned them their jobs.

Stickley got their advice on how to get promoted. Here are six factors they felt helps in becoming a chief.

1. Previous experience in all phases of police work is most important.

2. Education is also crucial. College degrees are important. Public administration makes the most sense as a course of study. Aside from degrees all kinds of courses related to supervision and management are helpful.

3. Superior performance is necessary. Women have to be quicker, sharper, more understanding, more mature, more innovative and enthusiastic about police work.

4. Goal-setting and determination to reach goals are essential.

5. Community involvement is recommended. Volunteer work related to police work is another way of getting training. Visibility strengthens support from others.

6. In contrast to the above five factors, which are all things to pay attention to, the last piece of advice is that being liked by the men *cannot* be a concern.

Stickley's (1987) report of a panel of women supervisors discussing "Women Supervising Men" likewise emphasizes the importance of studying and knowing rules, regulations, state statutes, city ordinances, and departmental policies. She recounts that Lt. Carolyn Burke, the highest ranking woman in a department of 4,000 (New York City's Transit Authority), advised that knowledge becomes confidence. Burke also advised emulating the best traits admired in other managers, but at the same time keeping one's own personality and sense of humor.

Mary Voswinkel, chief of police at Rice University in Houston, also has a list of principles for would-be administrators (1985). She says that any investment made toward administration will not be regretted. Here is some of what she advises.

1. Keep your business and personal lives separate.
2. Do not become one of the boys.
3. Treat everyone the same.
4. Accept responsibility for your own actions.
5. Keep business dealings at a high professional level.
6. Do not be disappointed when people do not support you.
7. Don't take criticism personally.
8. Understand that peers and subordinates are going to test you.
9. Keep tuned to institutional politics.
10. Find a mentor who understands you and is willing to listen.

Voswinkel is in favor of participatory management, of networking, and of developing one's own policing style. She says to find a department where the pluses outweigh the minuses and stick with it. On the other hand, if the minuses are intolerable, get out before your self-confidence is shaken. She says to take on additional responsibilities and learn the responsibilities of other jobs around you, so that when the opportunity to move up is there, you're prepared.

SUMMARY

Management matters. When a boss decides to increase the number of women by a complex of sensible, sensitive strategies, this intelligent commitment can make all the difference. Organizational commitment, starting at the top, brings about that critical mass of women and minorities necessary for all the bad effects of tokenism to disappear.

Departments will also retain more women when they adopt realistic maternity leave policies, institute flexible scheduling, and provide child care.

Other things being equal, women appear to be slightly less interested in promotion than men. Those who desire promotion typically feel less competent prior to supervisory training than do men. Men always seem to have the edge in self-reported self-confidence.

To be competent and accepted as leaders women must work their way up the ranks and pay their dues. Experience and perseverance are essential. Then women can adopt a modern participatory style of management, just as long as they can live with the knowledge that they are never going to be liked by everyone.

Chapter 11

IMPACT OF WOMEN ON POLICING

One impact of women and minorities on policing is that most agencies now have affirmative action plans and programs. Hochstedler (1984) reviewed what these plans consist of and says that they typically aim at four goals—recruitment, selection, retention, and promotion of greater numbers of minority group members, and to a far lesser extent, greater numbers of women.

The agencies start by pitching their recruitment advertising at both minority and nonminority audiences. They may follow this up by actively recruiting face-to-face at colleges and military bases, or by establishing cadet programs where they attempt to recruit minorities and females to the regular police service.

Then, some agencies have redesigned their selection criteria to remove requirements unrelated to policing and suspected of barring minorities and/or females. For example, some departments have eliminated rigid height and weight requirements, others have dispensed with portions of the physical agility test such as chinups, and still others changed the weight or size of revolvers used to qualify as a marksman. Some agencies have changed the content of the written exam, some have relaxed automatic disqualification of anyone with a misdemeanor conviction.

The final organizational effort evaluated by Hochstedler was the bottom line—selecting qualified minorities and women while underselecting qualified nonminority males. Hochstedler concluded that only this last effort, that is, *quota hiring*, "works," makes a difference. Only by using identical selection criteria but insisting on the hiring of minorities have agencies produced tangible affirmative action results. Simply relaxing earlier standards did not produce greater numbers of minorities. And the interesting thing was that if an agency had a hiring quota, it could keep a very high educational requirement or a very stringent disqualification-for-criminal-record, and it would still meet its affirmative action goal for hiring racial minorities.

The problem was that not a single agency of the fifteen Hochstedler studied had hiring quotas for females.

Thus, if an agency is *committed* to employing more women, using a hiring quota with all the connotations of "reverse discrimination" it implies, is the way to achieve that goal. Second, the agency must set high standards of employment so that women are known to be qualified. Third, it should simply pass or fail candidates, not rank them. And last, from the pool of qualified candidates, selection must be by chance except that women have a greater chance of selection in accord with the hiring quota. At the time Hochstedler gathered her data, the summer of 1981, women officers were five percent of the workforce in these agencies, a long way off from the percentage of women in the general workforce, which might be an appropriate affirmative action goal.

Another impact women have had is upon those police managers who committed their agencies to affirmative action. Once committed, they won't go back. Most state and local governments are refusing to alter their programs to hire and promote minorities and women, even though the Reagan administration asked them to ("State, local," 1985).

The Department of Justice made an expansive interpretation of a Supreme Court ruling and sent letters to 53 jurisdictions saying that they were required to modify their affirmative agreements. That decision, *Memphis Firefighters vs Stotts,* found that race cannot be taken into consideration during layoffs if an employer has a bona fide seniority system.

But when the Bureau of National Affairs wrote the 53 jurisdictions, asking "Do you plan to file a joint motion with the Justice Department seeking to alter your existing consent decree by abolishing hiring and promotion goals and timetables, as requested by the Department of Justice," only three said "yes." They were the Arkansas State Police, the Buffalo NY Fire and Police, and Wichita Falls, Texas police.

Do we know of any impact of women upon men police at a more personal level? Not beyond the level of the observational and interview study.

Susan Martin (1980) rode along with and interviewed 27 men and 28 women officers in Washington, DC back in 1975–76 for her doctoral dissertation. She thus gained firsthand knowledge of how women officers impact men officers' behavior.

The men told her that when they had women partners, they were more cautious, less likely to go all out, and took fewer risks. By their own admission the men's patrol behavior was restrained by having a woman along. The men also reluctantly admitted women sometimes restrained and cooled down angry male citizens. Because it wouldn't be chivalrous to hit or curse a woman officer, some men were less likely to injure male officers as well (p. 93).

Having women around the stationhouse made the men less aggressive to one another, less likely to threaten each other and get into fistfights to settle arguments. At the same time that men were more restrained about anger, the emotional reserve they maintained toward one another was threatened by women who were more likely to express affection and dependency, and thus possibly make a man's emotional control falter. The presence of women also made men not swear so much and inhibited them from telling off-color stories and bragging about their sexual prowess (p. 100).

Another impact of women officers was that they caused men to have more than one attitude toward women in policing, that is, attitudes other than those of "the traditionals." Traditional men strongly opposed women on patrol because they were physically weaker and lacked aggressiveness. Now, there were also "moderate" men who believed women had the right to equality of opportunity. And there was a minority of "modern" men who saw aggression as undesirable in many situations and who liked working with women because they were more empathic and tactful and acted as a restraining influence on men (pp. 102–108).

We will now take a look at the major areas where women might have made an impact—recruitment, selection, training, and performance.

RECRUITMENT AND SELECTION

Maher (1984) has written a critical review of PATs, physical agility tests, which concludes that PATs do not measure essential elements of police work, but rather peripheral elements that legally cannot be defended. Further, PATs have adverse impact on women, just as did minimum height and weight standards that have been found discriminatory and therefore proscribed by Title VII.

Among the PATs he lists (which must be done in a certain time limit) are scaling a wall, swimming a prescribed distance, running a set distance, broad jumping a set distance, running an obstacle course, and walking a beam several feet off the ground.

At the heart of Maher's doubts about PATs is the true nature of police work. He tells us it is far more tranquil than police officers perceive it to be. He says that the number of manhours expended per officer for "index crime" is less than 2 percent of total manhours per year. He reminds us that in most assaults, officers are not alone, but working together. Further, typically they use defensive weapons such as batons. And if they do have to run after suspects, it is at their sole discretion, and in so doing, they go as a team, helping one another climb walls and get around obstacles.

If apprehending combative suspects is that important, Maher says, departments should provide weaponless defense training and require that all officers demonstrate their proficiency on a regular basis rather than have a PAT. Weaponless defense training provides job related skills and does not have the adverse impact against women that PATs do. Similarly, rather than have a PAT that does not indicate a person's true physiological condition, departments should have preventive physical conditioning programs which require all officers to stay fit and avoid heart conditions, the single greatest cause of early retirement.

When departments continue to use PATs as pre-employment selection procedures, though, there are effective ways to reduce their adverse impact upon women.

For example, both the Los Angeles Police Department (LAPD) and the Los Angeles County Sheriff's (LACS) Department have physical fitness training programs the aim of which is to get more women in shape to pass the physical agility test to become cadets. Kerstein (1982) described a "pre-CPA" class for women who want to enter LAPD's Crime Prevention Assistant (CPA) Program, which in turn is a pre-police academy program aimed mostly at improving women's fitness for the physical rigors of the police academy. The pre-CPA program offers physical training on a volunteer basis two nights a week and on Saturdays.

Likewise, the LACS department offers remedial classes evenings and Saturdays aimed at the specific events which women and men failed when they took the cadet pre-employment physical agility test (Hernandez, 1983). This test consists of events such as climbing a 6-foot wall, a 440-yard run, and crawling through simulated windows. Speed is very important. The seven events must be done in 2 minutes and 50 seconds. Women were slower and failed more events, but more of them attended the classes and they were as likely as the men to improve their performance. Hernandez noted that the program would be just as valuable as an in-service refresher course for existent sworn personnel.

The kinds of discrimination that police departments cannot get away with any more are the stuff of Potts' (1983) review of judicial decisions after the Equal Employment Opportunity Act of 1972 which amended Title VII of the Civil Rights Act of 1964.

For example, the courts ruled against a Maine police interviewer who always gave women low scores on the oral examination because he felt they were not rough and tough enough to handle physical situations. And the court also ruled against interviewers who asked women applying for parking meter jobs if they could participate in stakeouts and make unassisted arrests. There is, of course, no relationship between stakeouts and arrests and the job of writing citations and collecting money from parking meters.

In sex discrimination cases under Title VII a very common form of litigation has to do with the legitimacy of height and weight requirements. Standards which have a disparate impact on the sexes must be proved to be job relevant and necessary for safe and efficient job performance. Potts (1983) cites the 5'8" height requirement of the New York State Police which they retained after Title VII in order to keep the department all male. This height had been chosen using the argument that officers had to be able to fire a shotgun over the roof of a police car. This argument faltered when it was pointed out that the state's own training program taught that shooting over the roof of a car was the least desirable course of action to follow in a shoot-out.

Similarly, the Baltimore police department's 5'7" requirement, established in 1973 after Title VII took effect, was ruled to have disparate impact because it excluded from consideration 82 percent of the female population between 18 and 34, but only 25 percent of similarly aged males.

Townsey (1982b) reviewed data gathered in 1979 by the Police Foundation about the use of agility tests in selecting police officers. She reported that at that time 78 percent of the municipal and 91 percent of the state police agencies surveyed used a physical agility test for the hiring of both men and women.

Townsey felt that agility tests continue to be used to keep women out of policing. As long as such tests emphasize upper body strength, they will eliminate a highly disproportionate number of women applicants. However, the courts have invalidated tests such as pushups, situps, broad jumps and obstacle courses because of disparate impact upon women. For example, San Francisco had a test that was declared invalid because while 63 percent of males passed it, only 2 of 166 female applicants did.

Further, the test measured skills used in emergencies rather than the skills needed for general patrol work.

A good example of nondiscriminatory physical agility test procedure is that of the Miami Police Department. Townsey says this test is given before training at the academy. The same test is used for women and men and both sexes pass the test in proportionate numbers. If an applicant fails the test, he or she is placed on a six-week hold in which to success-fully complete the test. Ninety-five percent of those who initially fail pass the test on retake. The marked increase in women officers in Miami during the 1970s is due to the department changing its selection proce-dures to emphasize an applicant's *potential* for completing training.

And an example of six fairly reasonable physical agility factors are those in use in Maine ("Maine to hire," 1983). One, you have to be able to push a standard-size vehicle 12 feet. Two, conduct a simulated rescue of an injured child through a school bus window. Three, carry one end of a stretcher bearing a 175-pound mannequin 200 feet. Four, climb a flat-bed truck. Five, do 45 situps in 2 minutes. And six, run a mile and a half in 15 minutes.

TRAINING

Diane Pike (1985) did participant-observations for nine weeks at the Eastern Police Academy and for four months at the Midwestern Police Academy. She interviewed 19 instructors, 18 men and one woman. The class at Eastern had 32 men and 4 women, the class at Midwestern 33 men and 8 women.

She says the instructors contrasted the greater acceptance of women at the academy with their own, "real life" police departments. Their more positive view of women's acceptance at the academy might, she thought, reflect the instructors' view of "how it ought to be" and their attempt to present themselves as close to that model of behavior as possible. But she thought it also reflected genuinely greater acceptance on their part, perhaps because it is easier to be favorable toward students and recruits than it is toward partners in the real world of patrol.

Pike found, too, that some instructors recognized women police had extra problems because of tokenism and because male recruits had such exaggerated responses to them. Instructors commented on men recruits being flirty and making sexual jokes, and acknowledged that living in co-ed dorms was difficult because of the men's mental abuse.

The way a lecture which was supposed to sensitize male recruits to women's problems backfired underscores male instructors' greater acceptance. Rather than becoming sensitized, the men dismissed the guest lecturer as inexperienced and relying on "just statistics," and held on to the opinions they had before he came.

Incidentally, Pike offered an excellent example of how training can change when the instructor is a woman. A female instructor taught a sex offenses class. Because women are often credited with special skills in dealing with sex offense cases, while men are often told they need to be more sensitive, this detective made a special effort to break down such stereotypes. She told the men they could do sympathetic things for rape victims that women couldn't do, such as help victims feel that not all men were going to hurt them.

Tailored Physical Training

Mary Jo Patterson (1980), writing for the short-lived *Police Magazine,* called her article about the New Jersey State Police's all-female police class, "Training Tailored to Women." The thirty women who graduated from this 5-month training program in 1979 "taught" the instructors the following lessons:

1. An emphasis on karate and judo which use lower body strength and lifting progressively heavier weights in one's spare time are two effective ways to bring women up to men's standards.

2. Practice at special exercises to strengthen grip overcomes women's weaker "weak" hand in firearms training.

3. Gradual breaking-in to boxing overcomes women's deep resistance to using force.

4. Daily weigh-ins and tests of strength teach women that physical fitness means cardiovascular strength, not "looking good."

5. Simulated stressful situations teach women recruits to handle stress as successfully as men recruits do.

6. Increasing the distance between women in running-in-formation exercises eliminates stumbling, falling, and foot injuries.

7. Low shoes rather than high-top sneakers cut women's foot injuries to almost zero.

It was not until the state police trainers accepted that they needed to learn new techniques and improvise and modify as they went along, that women were able to successfully complete New Jersey trooper training. In the previous class there had been 13 women, none of whom graduated.

Robert Lindsey (1982), defensive tactics instructor, reviewed several ways for training officers to insure the survival of women officers. First, trainers must make women develop a strong positive mental attitude toward their abilities. Second, women must be taught a keen awareness of who they are, where they are, what they are doing, and with whom they are dealing.

Third, women must be taught that, through awareness and quick reaction time, they can avoid an attack or delay an attack until they are in a better position to overcome it. Fourth, running and jumping rope should be incorporated into women's lives so that they can maintain a conditioned cardio-vascular system. And fifth, sensible calisthenics and weight training are needed to develop womens' upper body strength.

Sixth, "quality techniques" of dealing with close quarter confrontations must be taught, techniques that women can practice in class and after class. Women should learn techniques for using the baton, handcuffing, and weapon retention.

Lindsey's point was that viable alternatives exist to women relying totally on their (lesser) physical strength to overcome violent resistance and it's up to training officers to teach them these alternatives.

Additional Psychological Training

Among the 25 California women studied by Wexler and Logan (1983) were six training officers. Inadequate training was the top "organizational stressor" cited by the whole sample. In addition to male trainers being hostile and trying to harass female recruits into resigning, actual training was inappropriate and inadequate for women, especially physical training and assertiveness training. When the women trainers had women to train, they helped them with the problem of upper body strength. And unlike male field training officers who would step in and do the job if a female hesitated, the women trainers would walk away from the women, forcing them to do the job by themselves. But these special efforts were made on an informal basis, in contrast to the following program.

Staff members at the Southeast Florida Institute of Criminal Justice in Miami when approached by Sally Gross (1984) about her support program for women recruits had only one criticism to make, how come it wasn't being done for men recruits as well? Apparently her experimental project was so successful that institute administrators decided they would offer voluntary support groups for all recruits. The goals of these groups are to reduce intrapsychic and interpersonal stress and give recruits a sound foundation for positive mental health throughout their careers.

Just how did Sally Gross's group for women recruits operate? It was designed to counteract disillusionment with male peers and lack of self-confidence that women often experience during training. It was based on the notion that women can learn best how to maintain self-esteem and sex-role identity from other women, including veteran female officers. It was hoped that the support network which formed would be used in the future as a stress reducer. Role-modeling by veteran women officers was its cornerstone.

The issues the women dealt with were:

1. How to be a police officer with a balance of "feminine" and "masculine" qualities and behaviors. Getting to know respected women who used all aspects of their personalities in policing was essential.

2. How to be a wife, mother, and cop. How to cope with multiple roles and the different emotional reactions and behaviors called for at work and home. Hearing from veteran women how they mesh multiple roles and resolve issues with loved ones helped trainees with the same conflicts.

3. How to handle sexuality. Only by sharing perceptions, alternatives, and outcomes with other women who have confronted sexual issues can women recruits act professionally and responsibly with male colleagues.

4. How to handle competitiveness. Women need reinforcement from other women as they strive to excel and to overcome their ambivalence about competing with men and winning.

The elements of a voluntary support group include meeting (ideally) weekly for an hour and a half. The group leader should have police experience. At each meeting a different woman veteran officer leads the discussion. The veterans should be "good cops," married, single, divorced, with and without children. They should talk about personal problems, coping mechanisms, and resolution of issues such as assertiveness versus aggressiveness, male egos, fear of fighting, showing initiative, loss of femininity.

Gross mentioned a four-hour, mandatory, pre-academy orientation for the women in one class that was successful in developing the trust essential to self-disclosure and led to the women's long-term commitment to help other women. She also mentioned a meeting that another class had with their training advisors after graduation in which they shared feelings and suggestions for improving training. Having the women express their concerns directly to instructors was a good assertive exercise and gave them a sense of effecting systemwide change in the police.

Additional Skills Training

Morash (1986, p. 291) says several researchers at Michigan State University have been studying women police for some years through participant observation, attending training meetings, and holding interviews. Their initial findings are that women police take special actions to accomplish objectives important to them. One of their objectives was better training in the special skills needed to work with cases of child neglect, child abuse, and sexual assault. Morash says both individuals and statewide women's groups sponsored many types of training to compensate for the failure of police departments to fully meet the needs of both women and men.

Another place where women have championed the cause of better training is through police unions, where they also press for better working conditions and adequate maternity benefits.

The Spouse Academy

The Spouse Academy conducted by the Colorado Springs Police Department is a tribute to the ever-growing numbers of women police officers. Throughout their article, Ricks and Munger (1988) are careful to refer to the recruit officer as he/she and to recruits' spouses as spouses, not wives. Police husbands, they say, face the same problems as police wives plus the additional stress of having a wife in a traditionally male profession. The Spouse Academy, consequently, is designed for spouses of both sexes.

There are several features to the Academy which are particularly responsive to women recruits' needs. For example, the academy is held in the evening in recognition of the fact that so many spouses are employed. The academy provides child care! Thus, women recruits can do their homework and study for tests while their children go off with their husbands to the academy.

Aspects of the curriculum that might be particularly helpful to husbands are instruction in how new recruits react to their first homicide and suicide, how they may react after using deadly force, and how they can be expected to go through macho and cynical stages just as all rookies do.

KEEPING FIT

One side effect of agencies raising the issue of women's physical strength for police work has been the recognition that policing is largely a sedentary occupation. Michael Charles (1982, 1983) has written two articles on the necessity of agencies adopting individualized exercise programs to maintain acceptable fitness levels in veteran officers of all ages. Unless workers in sedentary occupations exercise several times weekly, they do not have the physical reserves to perform in emergency situations and are costly to employers.

He recommends for all police officers both continuous anaerobic exercise, such as weight training, and aerobic exercise such as jogging, walking, hiking, swimming, or basketball. All police officers should exercise at least three times a week for about 45 minutes. Sex and age have to be taken into account in any exercise program. For example, aging hinders trainability, and women can't reach the same plateau of fitness as men. Yet, Charles reminds us, even though there are basic physiological differences in physical strength between the sexes, trained female athletes are physiologically superior and fitter than nonathletic men. Women can be trained to satisfactorily perform heavy work, they have successfully been trained in military and police programs, and physically fit women can work as well as fit men in hot environments.

Charles recommends that departments develop individualized programs tailored to each officer's needs and interests. He firmly believes that women can train themselves to achieve a level of fitness well within the demands of their profession, and have the necessary reserves to pull accident victims out of cars, exchange blows with combative suspects, chase fleeing offenders on foot, climb fences, and push or pull stalled vehicles in emergency situations.

The documented benefits of continued fitness for the police are reduced incidence of coronary heart disease (very high among police), slowing of the aging process, increased longevity, reduced injuries on and off duty, decreased worker's compensation, decreased worker absenteeism, and financial savings to the employer.

Women have been found to have more injuries during cadet training than men, even when the women were in comparatively better shape prior to that training. Regali (1988) reports that 39 percent of 23 women between age 20–29 sustained injuries during the first four weeks at the Criminal Justice Academy versus 18 percent of 159 men of the same age. These injuries occurred in the academy's combination running and calisthenics course. The most common injuries were knee injuries, sprains, and muscle and ligament pulls.

The only pre-training measures that differentiated the women who subsequently got injured from the women who didn't were that the injured had a higher resting heart rate and weaker leg press strength. The 20–29 year old men, however, who got injured were in noticeably poorer shape than the men who did not get injured. The injured men came in with more body fat, less absolute strength in the upper body, less dynamic strength in the abdomen, and difficulty with the 1.5 mile run. Predispositions to injury were Regali's concern: After training, would out-of-shape officers get injured more often? Make more workmen's compensations claims? He warned police administrators that after keeping physically fit was as important for preventing injuries after graduation as it was during training.

PERFORMANCE EVALUATION

The courts since Title VII have clarified for the police how they may not discriminate against women when it comes to promotion. Potts' (1983) review of court cases included a Virginia county that excluded women from patrol but required one year of patrol for transfer to the investigation division. In order to open the whole department to women, the one year of patrol prerequisite was waived for female sworn officers who had more than a year of police experience in any division. Men officers protested and the department capitulated and retroactively imposed the year of patrol requirement and demoted the women who had been promoted. The courts rejected the department's contention that it was only trying to remedy its earlier improper action.

Similarly, the court was not impressed by a chief of police who asked a woman applicant for promotion how her family felt about her being a police officer and whether she was afraid. He denied her promotion and her request to transfer to patrol and opined that it was too bad there were no openings in the youth bureau. His biggest mistake, however, was telling human rights investigators that women shouldn't be sergeants (Potts, 1983).

Crime rates, clearance of crime rates, and costs of service are the traditional criteria against which a police department measures itself. Citizens get very upset if crime rates go up and just as upset if the rates of clearance of reported crimes through arrests goes down. And the public would also like to keep the cost of police service down.

Steel and Lovrich (1987) set out to see if having more women in the service had any impact on these three indicators of police effectiveness. Of course, inasmuch as they collected their data in 1981, the percentage of female police officers in the 254 cities they surveyed was only 3.2 percent overall, which doesn't exactly represent quantum numbers. Most of these women were probably newly hired and of limited experience, not exactly prepared to exert much of an impact on the hard, cold effectiveness measures which can be found on FBI computer tapes.

Nonetheless, what Steel and Lovrich did was to create two comparison groups from an original set of 254 cities. One group had very few women and the other group had the highest percentages of women among their officers. The 34 cities with the highest utilization of women had a mean rate of 14 percent women; the 39 cities with the lowest utilization of women had a mean rate of .6 percent women.

For all three measures—crime rates, clearance of crime by arrest rates, and cost of operation—Steel and Lovrich found no differences between the cities who hired the most and the least women police. More women did not mean crime soared, arrests declined, and expenses went up. More women also did not mean that the incidence of crime went down, that arrests went up, and that there were savings in public funds. Women officers, in these proportions, using these measures of effectiveness, apparently made no difference at all.

However, it must be remembered that these women were of low rank and limited seniority. They could not be expected to have any more impact than newly hired and inexperienced men on the police organization. Secondly, Steel and Lovrich were looking at crime rates and clearance rates for the period 1970–80, when there were even fewer women than in 1981. (Only for the per capita cost of police services did they have data from 1981.)

If there is reason to believe that women will significantly change these three performance measures, we'll probably have to wait until there is more variability in proportions of women officers (say, a range from 5 to

40 percent) and until such time as we can look at an entire set of cities, not just the extremes.

PHILOSOPHY: PREVENTION VERSUS SUPPRESSION

Have women had any impact on the goals of the police organization? It looks as if they will in the future.

The New Blue Line by Jerome Skolnick and David Bayley (1986) has the subtitle "Police Innovation in Six American Cities." Skolnick and Bayley are a noted sociologist and political scientist who had the support of the National Institute of Justice and the Police Foundation for their book. They believe that the chief innovation in policing today is a philosophical one, that is, belief in the goal of positive crime prevention over the goal of reactive crime control.

The new innovative breed of cop is described as part blue knight and part social worker. These new cops no longer have an "us versus them" attitude toward the public but work side by side with the public to prevent crime (p. 210). Community-oriented crime prevention techniques are what Skolnick and Bayley's book is all about, in Santa Ana, Detroit, Houston, Denver, Oakland, and Newark.

There are four major elements to community-oriented policing (pp. 212–220). (1) *Police-community reciprocity* means police officers who genuinely focus on the needs of particular communities and adopt a service-oriented style. (2) *Areal decentralization of command* means many mini-stations and heightened identification of the police with particular neighborhoods. (3) *Reorientation of patrol* means foot patrol, a concerned human presence on the street, generating goodwill in neighborhoods and raising officer morale in the bargain. (4) *Civilianization* means hiring civilians to do much of the work of the police service. For example, Santa Ana's goal was to have a service that was 55 percent civilian and 45 percent sworn officers.

Women fit beautifully into these innovations in a number of ways. While Skolnick and Bayley only stimulated the following ideas, I don't think they would disagree with these points.

First, women officers are more likely to favor a service-oriented style and community-oriented prevention to begin with. Skolnick and Bayley describe the "creative customized police work" Officer Dagmar Lane provides out of her mini-station in Detroit's worst neighborhood, Cass Corridor (p. 65). They said she loves her assignment and digs deep into the community in ways that can't be done from a patrol car. They also describe the style of Sue Hoffman (p. 168) who patrols downtown Oakland and who says to suspected street drug dealers, "There's no legitimate reason for your being here. Please leave." *Please leave!* Straightforward, businesslike, authoritative, and polite. Foot patrollers who have a service-oriented style do not have to make arrests to preserve public order. They can often accomplish the same thing by admonishing people like a school teacher would.

Second, Skolnick and Bayley have a lot to say about police officers' "rooted unwillingness to change their traditional approach." The greatest obstacle to implementing a community-oriented crime prevention, they say, is the traditional police organization itself. They were hard put to think of an organization more resistant to change than the police. It is not easy to transform blue knights into community organizers, they mused (p. 211).

But women police officers aren't opposed to change. They aren't opposed to the new and different and challenging. They tend to be self-directing, initiative-taking, able-to-deal-with-all-sorts-of-people individuals. A neighborhood mini-station requires officers who can show concern over and over again for the petty, undramatic problems of ordinary people. Officers are now needed who are empathic, patient, understanding, and totally committed to crime prevention as what people really want the police to do.

Third, the police service as an organization, as an institution, is aware that it expresses *values* in the way it operates. Values are what policing has always been about, but today those values are spoken out loud and they are different. Skolnick and Bayley in reference to the six cities say police values now include service, community participation, fairness, prevention, concern for ethnic and economic diversity, cooperation, honesty, and openness to new ideas. Women are socialized to internalize these values more than men. And women are not going to think nostalgically back to the good old days when crime was controlled by the value, "Kick ass and then take names."

Fourth, *civilianization,* labeled the most far-reaching and controversial innovation Skolnick and Bayley encountered, has irrevocably demonstrated women's capabilities for police work—if what happened in Santa Ana applies to civilianization elsewhere. Because 86 percent of Santa Ana's civilians are women! These Police Service Officers, PSOs, are used in almost every aspect of police service. They wear uniforms, ride alone in patrol cars, take and investigate complaints, respond to crime reports not in progress, and do almost all of Santa Ana's traffic investigations. According to the department, the PSOs provide "equally qualified service" to sworn officers. And Skolnick and Bayley agreed (p. 26).

I think civilianization is controversial for men because it threatens the traditional notion of what a police officer does. It is controversial for me because Santa Ana's PSOs get 70 percent of a patrol officer's salary and no benefits (p. 26). They were probably accepted by the men and administration only because they were saving the department so much money (40 percent cost saving) and were regarded as paraprofessionals with less status than sworn officers who were the "real" professionals.

Thus, civilianization can have another, ominous for women side. A side which widens the gulf between what patrol*men* do and the services provided by women. A side which perpetuates the economic disparity between women's work and men's work.

Allison Morris (1987, pp. 148–149) discusses the twin goals of crime control versus social service vis-a-vis the integration of women and men into the same organization in the U.K. in 1975. Do we have a police *force* or a police *service?* U.K. police administrators feel the organization should be both, and some urge a return to specialization for women on the grounds that assimilation had resulted in inferior service in the social service areas because women are now doing the full range of police work. Other administrators, however, see that specialization should be made on the basis of individual talent and interest, not sex. Thus, special training to selected women *and* men should be given in social service activities such as dealing with rape victims.

FUTURE IMPACTS?

Research on the impact of women on policing has barely begun. We need research on how they have affected the goals of agencies toward prevention and conflict resolution. We need research on cooperative management that listens to customers, and blames faulty processes, not employees.

We need research on proactive, community-oriented patrol functions, research on women's capability at the full range of specialized function, from traditional (traffic, juvenile, prevention) to SWAT, motorcycle and helicopter team detail.

We need research on the career development of police officers:

What happens to women and men five, ten, twenty, and 30 years after selection?

How do women affect departments' accountability? Productivity? Responsiveness to the families of officers? Responsiveness to the community?

Chapter 12

RESEARCH DIRECTIONS FOR THE 1990S

Samuel Walker (1985) accuses police scholars of using a paradigm that is out of touch with the realities of the American police culture. That paradigm sees departments has having made little progress in increasing the representation of minorities and women and of being dominated by traditional attitudes and behavior of white males. Police reformers have often viewed these working class males as minimally educated, conservative, authoritarian, racially prejudiced, and the major cause of poor police-community relations.

Walker believes, instead, that progress has been made in many departments and, as a result, innumerable slow, incremental, unplanned changes have occurred in law enforcement agencies which have gone unnoticed by scholars and the general public. Unnoticed and unresearched. So few studies have been done, he says, that these incremental, "glacial" events have outstripped our state of knowledge about today's police.

EXPERT SUGGESTIONS

To remedy our lack of information, Samuel Walker suggested a host of research directions for the 1990s in his 1985 article. After considering them, we'll look at some other experts' suggestions.

Walker says we need more research on the factors responsible for the hiring of more women and minorities. How effective are different strategies in achieving equal employment opportunity goals? For example, how important is *minority group political power?* Does black political power translate into minority and female police employment? (Does female political power translate into minority and female police employment?)

How successful has *employment discrimination litigation* been? Employment discrimination suits, he says, have challenged virtually every aspect of police personnel practices in the past decade. But despite all this litigation, little empirical research on it has been done. Is litigation effective? Has it succeeded without overly harmful side effects? Sometimes letting "the lawyers handle it" means regression not progression. What's the evidence?

Third, to what extent is affirmative action progress associated with *administrative leadership,* with administrators, white or black, male or female, who are committed to equal employment opportunity?

Areas ripe for research, according to Walker, include:

1. **Police Performance.** Have minority and women officers improved performance and police-community relations? Walker feels that police researchers have been particularly insensitive to changes, apart from those on-the-job, which have come about because of hiring more minorities and women.

2. **Public Attitudes.** How has the general image of departments changed with increased minority and female employment? Do minority group perceptions of the police improve? Does minority quota recruitment affect the attitudes of white citizens? How does the use of women on visible patrol affect the attitudes of male and female citizens? Do these attitudes change over time or as a result of personal contact with women officers?

3. **Police Subculture.** What have been the effects of greater numbers of minority group members and women on the police culture? How does initial hostility toward women and blacks change over time? Do white, black, Hispanic, and women officers form informal cliques? Do they socialize together off duty? Do male and female blacks identify primarily in terms of race or sex? Do these patterns of interaction affect attitudes on law enforcement policy? Do departments become "balkanized" into competing groups, or do all officers get socialized into a common "police" outlook?

4. **Promotions.** Why do some departments make progress and others do not? Which of the factors—political power, litigation, administrative leadership—are associated with promoting minorities and women? How have peer judgments affected their promotion?

There are at least three areas where subjective judgments affect promotion: performance ratings by supervisors, assignment to deadend jobs versus jobs where officers can distinguish themselves, and the promotional interview before higher-ranking officers. How do race and sex affect these decisions?

We also need to explore the hypothesis that affirmative action is counterproductive and inevitably poisons relations among employees.

And the hypothesis that affirmative action succeeds depending on whether top management is hostile or supportive.

5. **Police Unions.** At what point does union leadership respond to the growing numbers of minorities and women? Is there a critical mass needed to alter the policies of a union?

These are just a few of the many unresolved issues related to the slow, long-term, glacial changes that police research has not yet addressed.

A Look at the Past: Charles and Parsons' 1978 List

No doubt Michael Charles and Kevin Parsons would agree with Walker that because so little research has been conducted, our knowledge about the police has been eclipsed by both slow-moving and fast-moving events. These two investigators concluded over a decade ago that what little research on women police existed, could be criticized on the basis of methodological design and statistical analyses. Samples were too small, study periods too short, and results too limited in application.

Charles and Parsons felt the direction of research on women should shift to "how can we best use them" from "whether or not we should." They recommended a list of seventy very specific and applied research projects with women officers as a point of departure for investigators. Reading over the list makes it abundantly clear that we do not know much more today than we did when the 1970s' major evaluation studies were completed.

Before turning to the 70 topics, however, it is worth repeating the basic questions they saw in four key areas: physical competence, women's roles, diffusion of violence, and training.

With respect to physical competence, they ask: What level of physical performance is necessary for police officers? How do we measure that competency? What training is necessary for that competency? How do you maintain it? And, if an officer can perform 99 percent of police functions, should we let a vital 1 percent that cannot be performed outweigh the 99 percent?

In the area of women officers' roles they ask: What is the "proper" role of women in law enforcement? How do you communicate that to male colleagues? To the public? To the women themselves?

Regarding "diffusion of violence," Charles and Parsons cite the studies which indicate that women have a calming effect on potentially violent confrontations. If this is so, or since this is so, how can violence be defused? How can everyone, male and female, be trained to do it?

Last, the training questions were: How stressful should academy training be? Should extra training be provided some recruits? How well do academies prepare women personnel?

Some of the chapters of this book provide broad topic areas into which to sort Charles and Parsons' seventy research topics, although there was nothing on their list that might be considered "personality," "job satisfaction," or "retention and promotion" studies.

1. **Background:** Here would go the studies Charles and Parsons' proposed to deal with previous work experience, performance of veterans, credit hours of college, race and sex, marital status, number of children and their ages, prior arrest record, spouse response to male-female patrols, and grades on civil service exams. Beyond simply knowing what women and men police are like, what is the impact of these background variables upon women's and men's performance?

2. **Values, Attitudes, Interests:** Charles and Parsons think that deference expected or demanded from others should be studied, as well as an officers' cooperativeness with parole and probation officers. They also propose studies of acceptance of responsibility, ability to work with a partner, and ability to take orders.

3. **Stress:** One of the 70 topics was "ability to cope with stressful situations."

4. **Performance and Style:** Over half of Charles and Parsons' suggested projects fall here. These studies would have either to do with positive performance indices or negative performance indices, and most of the data would be gathered from supervisors' files. Examples of positive performance measures are number of citations issued, conviction rates, number of court appearances, quality of arrests, supervisory ratings, number of incidents handled per shift, promptness, and ability to perform special agency assignments.

Examples of negative performance measures are number of sick days used, number of job related injuries, unbecoming conduct, sexual relations between partners, taking of unnecessary risks, disciplinary actions taken against one, in-service automobile accidents, and post-academy resignations.

Other performance measures are neutral: time on single and night patrol, work assignments, amount of backup received.

Three of the 70 projects had to do with physical competence and they would also belong here: aggression level of officers (use of force), ability to use firearms, and loss of physical conditioning.

5. **Perceptions of Performance:** Among the 70 projects were citizen satisfaction with police service, citizen complaints, community image of the agency, treatment afforded prisoners, officer attitude toward citizens, handling of male and female contacts, and handling of juveniles. Charles and Parsons also felt that male officers' overprotectiveness toward women should be studied, as well as dispatchers' screening of calls, male and female officers' perceptions of the woman officer's role, and preference for sex of partner.

6. **Impact of Women on Policing:** Charles and Parsons' training projects might fall here: academy scores both physical and academic, resignations from the academy, amount of time needed to acquire physical (aerobic and anaerobic) and technical (defensive driving and firearms) skills, probationary evaluation, and pre-employment interview ratings. Two projects dealing with the diffusion of violence might also fall here: ability to handle violent confrontations and ability to calm violent confrontations.

Other topics of investigation are not easy to categorize, and probably even harder to conduct—"degree of dedication," "street wisdom," and "quality of service" are three.

A Look at the Future: Gitchoff and Henderson's 1999 Concerns

I liked Gitchoff and Henderson's (1985) observation that in spite of the criminal justice discipline leaning toward quantitative analysis as its primary data-gathering tool, it was still necessary to combine professional studies, public proclamations, creative caricatures, common sense, and other resources to get a good description of police behavior. That certainly proved to be the case describing women officers' behavior!

Gitchoff and Henderson say that in 1999, the police will be more racially balanced and integrated, better educated, and that women and men will be more equally represented at all levels, from patrol to administration. That after decades of "proving their worth," minorities and women will have been accepted into the police family.

Assuming these experts are correct, the impact of women on the trends and changes predicted by Gitchoff and Henderson should make for some tantalizing research.

Here are several of their predictions for how the nature of policing will change in the next decade. In each case, the question that might be investigated is, how might greater numbers of women facilitate these events?

1. There is going to be much greater citizen involvement in policing, for example, neighborhood watch programs, involvement which demands that citizens perceive the police as trustworthy, honest, and serving their particular community interests.

2. The paramilitary model of the police organization will be replaced by a bureaucratic management. Sensitivity training will be rediscovered to combat the impersonality of large departments.

3. Police unions will gain more power and continue to focus on "bread and butter" issues, at the same time jeopardizing positive citizen perceptions with images of corruption and waste.

4. The mental health of the police will be more important. Sabbatical leaves, counseling, and paid tuition for advanced degrees will be used to combat stress.

5. Specialization will be encouraged and rewarded with merit raises so that specialists can forego promotion and still get top pay.

6. There will be wider use of devices that deliver a more humane response such as nets and tranquilizer guns.

7. Old paramilitary administration will be replaced by participatory management.

8. The mission of urban officers will be a proactive enforcement model focusing on crime prevention.

9. The nation's citizenry will contain a greater proportion of women.

10. The police will be the caretakers for nearly every social problem. They will be expected to be crime fighters at the same time that they must be social workers and crisis interventionists.

RESEARCH TO END BONES OF CONTENTION

There are some serious rifts of opinion about women in law enforcement that good research could help settle. Some bones of contention are philosophical, some practical. Some deeply affect morale within law enforcement; others deeply affect citizen perceptions of law enforcement.

The point is, facts should replace myths. Knowledge should replace prejudice. Research can and should aid a profession, and in the police service there are now *enough* women who have served *long enough* that data to resolve controversies exist. What we need is the will to get those data and to aid the profession by providing answers in areas of disagreement.

Here are some examples.

Few Arrests, Many Arrests: What Is Desirable?

Few arrests or many arrests? Which is better? It all depends on a department's performance goals. Then, depending on the goal, one style of policing may be more acceptable than another style.

Bloch and Anderson (1974) noted that one of the major differences in the performance of women and men officers was that the women made fewer arrests. During the first six months of 1973, on average, the men made 5 felony arrests to the women's 1, 11 misdemeanor arrests to the women's 4, and 50 moving traffic citations to the women's 21. Which raises questions such as these: Are the women producing too few arrests, or are the men producing too many? What kind of arrests are necessary? Which arrests are desirable? Is it better to be quick to arrest or better to warn off minor offenders?

A department must answer such questions before trying to motivate women to produce as many arrests and traffic citations as men, said Bloch and Anderson. They pointed out that one of the effects of having a substantial number of women in a department is that it will be less aggressive. The presence of women, they speculate, may stimulate increased attention to ways of avoiding violence and cooling violent situations without using force.

Training and Performance: What *Is* Job-Related?

Katharine van Wormer (1981) wrote a wry piece exploring the question, "Are males suited to police patrol work?" She concluded that many men in the police service were not suited for it, but that through more careful hiring practices and placing women in leadership and patrol positions, the situation could be alleviated.

van Wormer reached her conclusions on the basis of research literature and she carefully cited the sources for her lists of men's advantages and disadvantages on patrol. Men's advantages were four: superior physical strength, superior household arrangements (wife at home), aggressiveess, and sometimes relevant job experience in the military.

Men's disadvantages were numerous. Referring to research studies and expert opinion in the criminal justice field, van Wormer said men were more likely to generate complaints and provoke violence than women. Men were more likely to become involved in seriously unbecoming conduct which damages community relations. Men found it harder to get cooperation from the public. Men tended not to have the education women officers had. Men didn't write reports as well, and didn't pay enough attention to detail.

The most telling case van Wormer made, however, had to do with men's lack of acceptance of women officers, for example, not wanting a woman patrol partner. This she described as very destructive to good inter-police relations as well as to community relations. Overall police performance also suffered when men overprotected women partners, wouldn't treat them as equals, or make joint decisions with them.

Although van Wormer's article was written in a semi-jocular manner, it could be taken very seriously. Male resistance to women is clearly counterproductive, indeed destructive, to the police organization. van Wormer said we need different selection criteria for police officers as a first step. And, after that, performance judged on devotion to duty, not on the use of the club and the gun. She has given us two valid research directions for the 1990s — selection criteria and performance evaluation based on positive, productive organizational goals.

Similarly, Merry Morash (1986, p. 290) provided fruitful questions for future research on job performance. For example, in the past to ask if women could perform the job *just like* or *as well* as a man assumed first, that men do not differ from one another in their methods. Second, it assumed that men's methods were known to be the most effective. In the past to focus on performance as forcefulness and physical strength assumed that male stereotypes were appropriate for police work.

To lead us to strategies for improving the structure of police departments, and in order to assist people in bringing about positive change, Morash says we must pay attention to how women police see their own experiences and themselves as police officers. What are women police officers' perceptions and objectives? Do the sexes in fact differ in their opinions of the appropriate methods and objectives of policing? Do women try to shape police work to fit their own self-images? And what strategies do women use to change other people and departments so as to maximize their own and others' contributions?

Do Women or Men Receive Preferential Treatment?

Women police believe men get preferential treatment. Men police believe women get preferential treatment. What's the reality?

Weisheit (1987) suspected that many officers did not object to women per se, but to the preferential treatment they believed women got from the police organization. His suspicions found support. Seventy-one percent of the men thought women had greater career opportunities than the men in the police, and 83 percent thought women got more lenient treatment for misbehavior. The men believed that because of their sex, women got more special assignments (84 percent) and promotions (91 percent). If it were not for government pressure, 95 percent of the men said, few departments would hire women.

Are suspicions of preferential treatment behind the slow progress, across our border in Canada, made by women constables in the Royal Canadian Mounted Police ("RCMP making slow progress," 1988)? There were 852 women constables in Canada in 1986, about 6.5 percent of all constables, yet they were not accepted as equals. They were resented by many male colleagues. And some of the force's policies were responsible for not only having a negative effect on the attitudes of men officers, but, ironically, for presenting "a permanent career obstacle" to women in the Mounties.

How should preferential treatment be investigated? If the facts about special assignments, discipline, and promotion were presented, and, in fact, the evidence was that the sexes were treated equally, would those who believe otherwise give up their beliefs? Perhaps this is what should be studied: why do coworkers cling to erroneous beliefs about colleagues despite evidence to the contrary?

Can Women Be Effective Police Supervisors and Leaders?

A major stumbling block to women's advancement in policing is the traditional belief that women cannot lead men. That men will not respect women's supervision and won't follow their orders. That women do not possess the authority, strength, size, and political savvy that supervising officers and running a police organization requires.

However, some people feel that the first step towards "quality policing" today is "quality leadership," and quality leadership appears to require characteristics that women are more likely to develop than men because of their sex-role socialization.

Couper and Lobitz (1988) say that policing is now being influenced by the "quality and productivity" movement that is transforming American businesses. That the "new age" managerial skills are replacing "old age" organizing and controlling. That policing is also a business, whose customers are the citizens, and whose product is service, meaning everything from crime fighting and conflict management to safety and prevention programs.

Throughout their article they continually refer to the police *service* to underscore the "new style" of leadership required today. That style means teamwork (rather than individual effort and competitiveness), asking the customers what they want (rather than experts deciding for them), asking and listening to employees (rather than telling them what to do), bosses being coaches and teachers (not patriarchs and order-givers), trusting employees (not watching and controlling them), and looking at errors as caused by failed systems and processes that need improvement (not blaming employees).

If "new style" leadership is the direction in which police organizations are leaning, this is all the more reason to research the effectiveness of women as police managers and test the old assumptions that men prefer top-down, power-oriented leadership.

THE POLICE SERVICE IN THE
MIDST OF BASIC CULTURAL CHANGE

The studies reported in this book point to the great necessity for more research on reducing men officers' hostility toward women officers.

Weisheit and Mahan (1988, p. 150) report from a study of Weisheit's that 191 male state police officers held the following opinions: men would resent being supervised by women (85 percent agreed), women didn't show as much longterm commitment to policing as men did (81 percent agreed), using women extensively would create interpersonal conflict in the police department (65 percent agreed), and women have a difficult time being accepted by men (65 percent agreed). (Why 100 percent did not agree on that last item, that's the question!)

In any case, Weisheit and Mahan say the real problem is that men are concerned that women are given preferential treatment in hiring, assignments, and promotion. It's not that the men are against women;

they are primarily concerned that men be treated equitably. These men even believed that women had an easier time than men at the academy (53 percent agreement).

If belief in preferential treatment for women is the source of men's *hostility,* how do agencies reduce that hostility and avoid other adverse efforts?

Wexler and Logan (1983) concluded their analysis of the sources of stress in women officers by asking why men, especially the women's colleagues, behave as they do. Five of the most significant stressors in the lives of the women Wexler and Logan interviewed were related to male colleagues' negative attitudes toward them.

Wexler and Logan's explanation was that men police suffer from the increasingly negative attitudes of the general public toward them, at the same time that this public calls upon them to do more and more. They deal with this stress by scapegoating, taking out their frustration on women police. They may also question just how masculine they themselves are if women can move into this archetype of masculine occupations and do well.

If scapegoating is the basis for men's hostility, what can departments do to prevent it?

Joseph Balkin (1988) also asked, "why don't policemen like police-women?" Balkin noted that working side by side with women police does not change men's negative attitudes. He noted, in spite of numerous evaluation studies demonstrating that women can do the job, men police go right on believing that women cannot do it. Why and how do men maintain these beliefs is what Balkin sets out to explain.

His answer was that many men who become police officers grew up being severely disapproved of by their parents for not being manly. "Manly" meant strength, aggression, bravery, and superiority to women, especially at work. Such men get anxious if they can't exhibit these "manly" qualities. If they can't show others how manly they are, they become afraid that they are going to be disapproved.

Thus, if such men correctly perceived that women police were doing their jobs, competently, they would feel less manly, get anxious and fear disapproval. Quite simply, the men distort their perceptions; they do not perceive the women accurately. Instead, they see them as not strong or courageous, as not doing the job as well as men. And since there are many men who feel this way, they collectively reinforce their distorted views of women police. One reason men protect women police from dangerous situations, Balkin reasons, is to protect themselves from seeing how competent the women are.

Balkin was very pessimistic. He said it is useless to try to convince such men of women's ability. It would involve feeling anxious and recalling parents' disapproval, and then realizing that parental disapproval does not mean that other people, today, were going to disapprove of them. In Balkin's mind, there was no hope for men police raised by parents who disapproved of unmanliness.

He concluded that changes in the attitudes of men police will only come from changes in broad cultural values regarding childrearing and sex-role stereotypes.

The question is, what programs are there in the U.S. or elsewhere to help men deal with their resistance toward women officers? What kinds of psychological help or in-service training are effective? As I point out in reviewing Katharine van Wormer's (1981) article, men not accepting women officers is destructive to good intra-police relations. And the police service cannot afford to resist basic cultural changes occurring in broad society. Indeed, it should be progressive rather than lagging behind.

COMPLEMENTARINESS OF WOMEN AND MEN FOR POLICING

A number of writers have hinted that police work requires both women and men because of the socialized complementariness of their respective skills, values, interests, and personality traits. Complementariness is different from specialization. People who advocate specialization would say that each sex should do what it is best at. Women, for example, should do juvenile work, interview rape victims, and do searches of women. Men should do homicide investigations, ride motorcycles, and be on the SWAT team.

In contrast, believers in complementariness say both women and men should be trained as generalists and thereafter found side by side doing patrol work and side by side in all specialized units. Because complementariness means that every type of police work requires the perspectives and approaches of both women and men.

Phyllis Baunach and Nicole Rafter (1982, p. 346), as part of their advice as to how women and men officers can work productively together, refer to the qualities a man brings to police work that a woman doesn't have, and vice versa. Neither one has qualities socialized only in the other sex. But in the combination of their different qualities, they make an excellent police team.

Peter Horne (1980), too, seems to believe in the complementariness of the sexes for policing. He advocates sexually-integrated, one-man, one-woman units because of women's strengths in handling victims and family disturbances (p. 193). He notes that aggressive and physical policing are not the final definition of good policing, but that active listening, compassion, and human responsiveness are equally important characteristics (p. 114).

Likewise, Anthony Vastola (1980) seems to believe in complementariness in proposing an empirical way for managers to pair people up as patrol car partners. He said managers typically use their intuition or simply tell officers to choose their own partners. Productivity might go up, Vastola proposed, if instead partners were assigned on the basis of the ideal mix of human characteristics for getting the job done. Perhaps it would be more productive, for example, to put together an officer who leaned toward the human relations side of policing with one who leaned toward crime control. Or more productive to have a people-oriented officer teamed up with an officer who was most concerned about crime control.

Although no research has been done on just what mix would be most productive, Vastola presented a hypothetical portrait of what those ideal characteristics might be. Regarding politics, one officer was liberal, the other moderate. In personality, one was gregarious, the other conservative. And as far as sex was concerned? One was male, the other female. It was a hypothetical model, to be sure. But suggesting as he did, that the ideal mix of what it takes to be the most productive team, might be a male officer and female officer, is what complementariness is all about.

An important area where the sexes could complement one another is stress reduction. Brenda Washington (1981) notes that each sex gets socialized to reduce stress differently. Men learn to direct their energies toward physical activities and sports. Women learn to cry. *Both* are good approaches to stress reduction. Her implication is that men should learn that crying is an acceptable emotional outlet for them as well as women, and women should learn how to use physical activity and sports to reduce stress. In expressing emotional feeling men and women officers are complementary to each other physically and mentally. Neither sex is superior or inferior, she says, especially in terms of doing police work. It would be like arguing which is inferior or superior for the job of securing a door, the key or the lock—pointless.

THE LAST WORD

I find it remarkable that during the 1980s so little research on women police officers was conducted. Judging from the reception I got from the Seattle police officials from whom I asked for help, it *cannot* be laid to a suspicious and uncooperative police organization. Is the dearth of empirical articles due, instead, to researchers who dispair that without federal funding, what can possibly be done?

I would suggest that, in point of fact, very much can be done without federal funding. This book was done without financial support from anybody. There are mounds of archival data out there as a start. Files and files full of records on police selection, training, and performance. Piles and piles of application forms, personality test profiles, and ratings from interviews. There are hosts of questions police organizations would like to ask of those data. I think the academic community would find that if it cooperated with the police community in the pursuit of research, results could be produced that would satisfy practical concerns and theoretical issues at the same time. Where there's a will, there's a way.

On the afternoon of Officer Gail Cobb's funeral on September 24, 1974, Sergeant Mary Ellen Abrecht gave a talk to police administrators. She reminded them that the DC experiment had worked. That for two years and eight months, women had been on patrol and that they were now an integral part of patrol and every other division of the department. She said that the women had succeeded in spite of the problems of the men's overprotectiveness and stereotyping, and the women's lack of aggressiveness and confidence (Abrecht and Stern, 1976, p. 267–270).

Women police were there to stay. Their presence was serious. Gail Cobb's death should be a sober reminder to recruiters to care more about a women applicant's stamina and street savvy than her figure and face. Cobb's death should be a sobering influence on administrators who put untrained women on patrol hoping they would fail. Her death should be kept in mind by academy instructors tempted to let women slip through firearms and self-defense training without gaining adequate skills. Cobb's loss should be a sobering influence on senior patrol officers who treated rookie women as a joke and refused to give them the benefit of their experience (p. 268).

From all I can see, the organization nationwide did sober up and went on to recruit and train women, albeit in small numbers. But their numbers continue to grow, and there is no going back.

My last word, *my research direction for the 1990s,* is for studies which focus on women's street savvy and stamina, women's strengths and successes. How have women established their credibility? How have they changed the organization for the better? How far have they come since Gail Cobb proved that women are willing to pay their dues and share the life-and-death encounters men feel are so integral to the career of a police officer?

REFERENCES

Abrecht, Mary E., and Stern, Barbara L.: *The Making of a Woman Cop.* New York, William Morrow, 1976.

Aiken, Lewis R.: *Psychological Testing and Assessment,* 5th ed. Boston, Allyn and Bacon, 1985.

Ammann, Thomas R.: A peek into the future. *Police Chief, 48* (No. 5): 53–55, 1981.

Austin, Thomas L., and O'Neill, John J.: Authoritarianism and the criminal justice student: A test of the predispositional model. *Criminal Justice Review, 10:* 33–40, 1985.

Balkin, Joseph: Why policemen don't like policewomen. *Journal of Police Science and Administration, 16:* 29–38, 1988.

Baunach, Phyllis J., and Rafter, Nicole H.: Sex-role operations: Strategies for women working in the criminal justice system. In Rafter, Nicole H., and Stanko, Elizabeth A. (Eds.): *Judge, Lawyer, Victim, Thief: Women, Gender Roles, and Criminal Justice.* Boston, Northeastern University Press, 341–358, 1982.

Bell, Daniel J.: Policewomen: Myths and reality. *Journal of Police Science and Administration, 10:* 112–120, 1982.

Bell, Lucille M.: The unfair family affair. *Police, 12* (No. 6): 29–31, 1988.

Berg, Bruce L., and Budnick, Kimberly J.: Defeminization of women in law enforcement: A new twist in the traditional police personality. *Journal of Police Science and Administration, 14:* 314–319, 1986.

Berg, Bruce L., and Budnick, Kimberly J.: Defeminization of women in law enforcement: Examining the role of women in policing. In Kennedy, Daniel B., and Homant, Robert J. (Eds.): *Police and Law Enforcement, Volume V.* New York, AMS Press, 159–171, 1987.

Bloch, Peter, Anderson, Deborah, and Gervais, Pamela: *Policewomen on Patrol (Major Findings: First Report, Volume I).* Washington, DC, Police Foundation, 1973.

Bloch, Peter, and Anderson, Deborah: *Policewomen on Patrol: Final Report.* Washington, DC, Police Foundation, 1974.

Blumberg, Abraham S., and Niederhoffer, Elaine (Eds.): *The Ambivalent Force: Perspectives on the Police,* 3rd ed. New York, Holt, Rinehart and Winston, 1985.

Blumberg, Mark: Research on police use of deadly force: The state of the art. In Blumberg, Abraham S., and Niederhoffer, Elaine (Eds.): *The Ambivalent Force: Perspectives on the Police,* 3rd ed. New York, Holt, Rinehart and Winston, 340–350, 1985.

Breci, Michael G.: Police officers' values on intervention in family fights. *Police Studies, 10* (No. 4): 192–202, 1987.

191

Bureau of Labor Statistics. Police, detectives, and special agents. *Occupational Outlook Handbook, 1988–89 Edition.* Bulletin 2300. Washington, DC, U. S. Department of Labor, 262–264, April 1988 (a).

Bureau of Labor Statistics. *Occupational Projections and Training Data, 1988 Edition.* Bulletin 2301. Washington, DC, U. S. Department of Labor, April 1988 (b).

Buzawa, Eva S.: Determining patrol officer job satisfaction. *Criminology, 22* (No. 1): 61–81, 1984.

Carpenter, Bruce N., and Raza, Susan M.: Personality characteristics of police applicants: Comparisons across subgroups and with other populations. *Journal of Police Science and Administration, 15:* 10–17, 1987.

Chance, Sue: Partners in life. *Police, 12* (No. 6): 32–35, 1988.

Charles, Michael T.: The performance and socialization of female recruits in the Michigan State police training academy. *Journal of Police Science and Administration, 9:* 209–223, 1981.

Charles, Michael T.: Women in policing: The physical aspect. *Journal of Police Science and Administration, 10:* 194–205, 1982.

Charles, Michael T.: Police training: A contemporary approach. *Journal of Police Science and Administration, 11:* 252–263, 1983.

Charles, Michael T., and Parsons, Kevin: Female performance in the law enforcement function: A review of past research, current issues and future potential. *Law and Order, 26* (No. 1): 18–74 (not continuous), 1978.

Christophe, Mariette: Androgynous management. *WomenPolice, 22:* 6–7, 1988.

Cooper, Mary: The best of both worlds. *Campus Law Enforcement Journal, 15* (No. 1): 18, 21, 1985.

Couper, David C., and Lobitz, Sabine H.: Quality leadership: The first step towards quality policing. *Police Chief, 55* (No. 4): 79–84, 1988.

Coyne, John P.: The lady is no tramp. *The National Centurion, 2:* 37–40, 1984.

Dallas police reject plea to link women with men on patrol. *Crime Control Digest, 18* (No. 29): 3–4, July 23, 1984.

Darrow, Terri: Facing challenges: A way of life. *Police, 12* (No. 3): 40–42, 1988.

Davis, Christine A.: "Ann Roling: Walking in another set of shoes." *Campus Law Enforcement Journal, 12* (No. 4): 34–36, 1982.

Davis, James A.: Perspectives of policewomen in Texas and Oklahoma. *Journal of Police Science and Administration, 12:* 395–403, 1984.

Diskin, Carolyn M.: Attitude and fitness achievement levels of female law officers. *Police Chief, 52* (No. 11): 32–34, 1985.

Doerner, William G.: Perceived seriousness of child abuse and neglect. *Criminal Justice Review, 12:* 13–20, 1987.

Dorsey, R. Rita, and Giacopassi, David J.: Demographic and work-related correlates of police officer cynicism. In Kennedy, Daniel B., and Homant, Robert J. (Eds.): *Police and Law Enforcement, Volume V.* New York, AMS Press, 173–188, 1987.

Dreifus, Claudia: 'People are always asking me what I'm trying to prove . . . ' *Police Magazine, 3* (No. 2): 18–25, 1980.

Ellison, Katherine W., and Genz, John L.: *Stress and the Police Officer.* Springfield, IL, Charles C Thomas, 1983.

Feinman, Clarice: Women in law enforcement. In Feinman, Clarice: *Women in the Criminal Justice System*, 2nd ed. New York, Praeger, 79–103, 1986.

Ferrier, James E.: Is there a typical female university police officer? *Campus Law Enforcement Journal, 15* (No. 1): 26–29, 1985.

Fleming, Alice: *New on the Beat: Woman Power in the Police Force*. New York, Coward, McCann, and Geoghegan, 1975.

Fry, Lincoln J.: A preliminary examination of the factors related to turnover of women in law enforcement. *Journal of Police Science and Administration, 11:* 149–155, 1983.

Fry, Louis W., and Greenfield, Sue: An examination of attitudinal differences between policewomen and policemen. *Journal of Applied Psychology, 65:* 123–126, 1980.

Garrison, Carole G., Grant, Nancy, and McCormick, Kenneth: Utilization of police women. *Police Chief, 55* (No. 9): 32–35, 69, 72–73, 1988.

Gitchoff, G. Thomas, and Henderson, Joel: What goes around, comes around: Policing America, 1999. In Blumberg, Abraham S. and Niederhoffer, Elaine (Eds.): *The Ambivalent Force: Perspectives on the Police*, 3rd ed. New York, Holt, Rinehart, and Winston, 419–424, 1985.

Glaser, Debra F., and Saxe, Susan: "Psychological preparation" of female police recruits. *FBI Law Enforcement Bulletin, 51* (No. 1): 5–7, 1982.

Gelernter, Carey Q.: Her "respectable" career path wasn't quite all in the family. *Seattle Times,* K2, May 7, 1989.

Golden, Kathryn: Women as patrol officers: A study of attitudes. *Police Studies, 4* (No. 3): 29–33, 1981.

Golden, Kathryn M.: The police role: Perceptions and preferences. *Journal of Police Science and Administration, 10:* 108–111, 1982 (a).

Golden, Kathryn M.: Women in criminal justice: Occupational interests. *Journal of Criminal Justice, 10:* 147–152, 1982 (b).

Grennan, Sean A.: Findings on the role of officer gender in violent encounters with citizens. *Journal of Police Science and Administration, 15:* 78–85, 1987.

Gross, Sally: Women becoming cops: Developmental issues and solutions. *Police Chief, 51* (No. 1): 32–35, 1984.

Hamilton, Mary E.: *The Policewoman: Her Service and Ideals*. New York, Frederick A. Stokes, 1924. (Arno Press and the New York Times, New York, 1971, reprint edition)

Hansen, Jo-Ida C., and Campbell, David P.: *Manual for the SVIB-SCII, Strong-Campbell Interest Inventory, Form T325*, 4th ed. Palo Alto, Consulting Psychologists Press, 1985.

Hauptman, Barbara J.: Proposed maternity leave package for the Omaha Police Division together with "maternity leave" benefits of eight other departments, 1989. (Available from Sgt. Barbara Hauptman, 505 South 15th Street, Omaha, NE 68102-2769)

Hernandez, Ernie, Jr.: Females in law enforcement: Femininity, competence, attraction, and work acceptance. *Criminal Justice and Behavior, 9:* 13–34, 1982.

Hernandez, Ernie: Physical agility remedial training. *Journal of Police Science and Administration, 11:* 42–45, 1983.

Higginbotham, Jeffrey: Sexual harassment in the police station. *FBI Law Enforcement Bulletin, 57* (No. 9): 22–29, 1988.

Higgins, Lois L.: *Policewoman's Manual.* Springfield, IL: Charles C Thomas, 1961.

Hochstedler, Ellen: Impediments to hiring minorities in public police agencies. *Journal of Police Science and Administration, 12:* 227–240, 1984.

Hochstedler, Ellen, Regoli, Robert M., and Poole, Eric D.: Changing the guard in American cities: A current empirical assessment of integration in twenty municipal police departments. *Criminal Justice Review, 9:* 8–14, 1984.

Hoffman, Dennis E., Little, William A., and Perlstein, Gary R. Racial minorities and women workers in a big city police department: A case study in the elusiveness of affirmative action. *Criminal Justice Review, 5* (No. 2): 22–33, 1980.

Homant, Robert J.: The impact of policewomen on community attitudes toward police. *Journal of Police Science and Administration, 11:* 16–22, 1983.

Homant, Robert J., and Kennedy, Daniel B.: A content analysis of statements about policewomen's handling of domestic violence. *American Journal of Police, 3:* 265–283, 1984.

Homant, Robert J., and Kennedy, Daniel B.: Police perceptions of spouse abuse: A comparison of male and female officers. *Journal of Criminal Justice, 13:* 29–47, 1985.

Horne, Peter: *Women in Law Enforcement,* 2nd ed. Springfield, Charles C Thomas, IL, 1980.

Hunt, Raymond G., McCadden, Karen S., and Mordaunt, Timothy J.: Police roles: content and conflict. *Journal of Police Science and Administration, 11:* 175–184, 1983.

Janus, Samuel S., Janus, Cynthia, Lord, Lesli K., and Power, Thomas: Women in police work—Annie Oakley or Little Orphan Annie? *Police Studies, 11* (No. 3): 124–127, 1988.

Jones, Catherine A.: *Predicting the Effectiveness of Police Officers.* Unpublished master's thesis, San Diego State University, 1987 (a).

Jones, Catherine A.: Unpublished raw data on sex differences from *Predicting the Effectiveness of Police Officers,* 1987 (b).

Jones, Sandra: *Policewomen and equality: Formal policy versus informal practice?* London, Macmillan, 1986.

Kennedy, Daniel B., and Homant, Robert J.: Nontraditional role assumption and the personality of the policewoman. *Journal of Police Science and Administration, 9:* 346–355, 1981.

Kennedy, Daniel B., and Homant, Robert J.: Attitudes of abused women toward male and female police officers. *Criminal Justice and Behavior, 10:* 391–405, 1983.

Kerstein, Alan: Crime prevention assistants: The bridge between recruitment and training of female officers. *Police Chief, 49* (No. 8): 50–51, 1982.

Koenig, Esther J., and Juni, Samuel: Attitudes toward policewomen: A study of interrelationships and determinants. *Journal of Police Science and Administration, 9:* 463–474, 1981.

Kuntz, Gregory: Development and implementation of Glynco's physical assessment test. *Police Chief, 52* (No. 11): 23–30, 1985.

Lawson, Chris: Dress right . . . dress. *The National Centurion, 1* (No. 5): 44–47, August 1983.

Lester, David, Gronau, Fred, and Wondrack, Kenneth.: The personality and attitudes of female police officers: Needs, androgyny, and attitudes toward rape. *Journal of Police Science and Administration, 10:* 357–360, 1982.

Lindgren, Sue A.: The cost of justice. In *Report to the Nation on Crime and Delinquency,* 2nd ed. Washington, DC, Bureau of Justice Statistics, Department of Justice, March 1988.

Lindsey, Robert K.: Officer survival: The female officer. *Law and Order, 30* (No. 7): 54–57, 1982.

Linn, Edith, and Price, Barbara R.: The evolving role of women in American policing. In Blumberg, Abraham S., and Niederhoffer, Elaine (Eds.): *The Ambivalent Force: Perspectives on the Police,* 3rd ed. New York, Holt, Rinehart and Winston, 69–80, 1985.

Love, Ken, and Singer, Ming: Self-efficacy, psychological well-being, job satisfaction and job involvement: A comparison of male and female police officers. *Police Studies, 11* (No. 2): 98–102, 1988.

Maher, Patrick T.: Police physical ability tests: Can they ever be valid? *Public Personnel Management Journal, 13:* 173–183, 1984.

Maine to hire more female troopers. *Criminal Justice Newsletter, 14* (No. 13): 5, June 20, 1983.

Martin, Carol A.: Women police and stress. *Police Chief, 50* (No. 3): 107–109, 1983.

Martin, Catherine A., McKean, H. E., and Veltkamp, Lane J. Post-traumatic stress disorder in police and working with victims: A pilot study. *Journal of Police Science and Administration, 14:* 98–101, 1986.

Martin, Molly: Rose Melendez, police officer (interview). In Martin, Molly (Ed.) *Hard-Hatted Women: Stories of Struggle and Success in the Trades.* Seattle, Seal Press, 71–80, 1988.

Martin, Susan. E.: *Breaking and Entering: Policewomen on Patrol.* Berkeley, University of California Press, 1980.

Masters, Ruth E., and Rasmussen, Judith Y.: Law enforcement: A woman corrections professor and a woman reserve officer's view. *Police Chief, 50* (No. 1): 61–66, 1983.

McCarron, Ann K.: Gender differences really differences in personality. *Campus Law Enforcement Journal, 15* (No. 1): 17, 25, 1985.

Meagher, M. Steven, and Yentes, Nancy A.: Choosing a career in policing: A comparison of male and female perceptions. *Journal of Police Science and Administration, 14:* 320–327, 1986.

Mellor, Earl F.: Weekly earnings in 1986: A look at more than 200 occupations. *Monthly Labor Review, 110* (No. 6): 41–46, 1987.

Milton, Catherine H., Abramowitz, Ava, Crites, Laura, Gates, Margaret, Mintz, Ellen, and Sandler, Georgette: *Women in Policing: A Manual.* Washington, DC, Police Foundation, 1974.

Morash, Merry: Understanding the contributions of women to police work. In Radelet, Louis A. *The Police and the Community,* 4th ed. New York, Macmillan, 290–292, 1986.

Morash, Merry, and Greene, Jack R.: Evaluating women on patrol. *Evaluation Review, 10:* 230–255, 1986.

Morris, Allison: *Women, Crime and Criminal Justice.* Oxford, U. K., Basil Blackwell, 1987.

Moss, Philip I.: Employment gains by minorities, women in large city government, 1976–83. *Monthly Labor Review, 111* (No. 11), 18–24, 1988.

NYPD gears up for HQ-based child care. *Law Enforcement News, 14* (No. 284): 1, 7, 1989.

O'Block, Robert L., and Abele, Vicki L.: The emerging role of the female detective. *Police Chief, 47* (No. 5): 54–55, 69, 1980.

Ott, E. Marlies: Effects of the male-female ratio at work: policewomen and male nurses. *Psychology of Women Quarterly, 13:* 41–57, 1989.

Out-of-wedlock pregnancy cannot serve as basis for termination. *Police Chief, 53* (No. 2): 53, 1986.

Outstanding woman chief is honored by her peers. *Campus Law Enforcement Journal, 13* (No. 5): 45, 1983.

Patterson, Mary Jo: Training tailored to women. *Police Magazine, 3* (No. 5): 23–29, 1980.

Pendergrass, Virginia E., and Ostrove, Nancy M.: A survey of stress in women in policing. *Journal of Police Science and Administration, 12:* 303–309, 1984.

Pike, Diane L.: Women in police academy training: Some aspects of organizational response. In Moyer, Imogene L. (Ed.): *The Changing Roles of Women in the Criminal Justice System: Offenders, Victims, and Professionals.* Prospect Heights, IL, Waveland Press, 250–270, 1985.

Pogrebin, Mark R.: The changing role of women: Female police officers' occupational problems. *Police Journal, 59:* 127–133, 1986.

Poole, Eric D., and Pogrebin, Mark R.: Factors affecting the decision to remain in policing: A study of women officers. *Journal of Police Science and Administration, 16:* 49–55, 1988.

Portland police chief resigns; was sole big-city female chief. *Criminal Justice Newsletter, 17* (No. 12): 1–2, June 16, 1986.

Potts, Lee W.: Equal employment opportunity and female criminal justice employment. *Police Studies, 4* (No. 3): 9–19, 1981.

Potts, Lee W.: Equal employment opportunity and female employment in police agencies. *Journal of Criminal Justice, 11:* 505–523, 1983.

Powers, Matthew T.: Employment motivations for women in policing. *Police Chief, 50* (No. 11): 60–63, 1983.

Price, Barbara R.: A study of leadership strength of female police executives. *Journal of Police Science and Administration, 2:* 219–226, 1974.

Radelet, Louis A.: *The Police and the Community,* 4th ed. New York, Macmillan, 1986.

RCMP making slow progress in accepting female officers. *Crime Control Digest, 22* (No. 14): 7, April 4, 1988.

Regali, Joseph E.: Athletic injuries: A comparative study of municipal/county basic police cadets at the Maine Criminal Justice Academy. *Journal of Police Science and Administration, 16:* 80–83, 1988.

Remmington, Patricia W.: Women in the police: Integration or separation? *Qualitative Sociology, 6:* 118–135, 1983.

Ricks, Paul C., and Munger, James D.: The forgotten recruit—training the police spouse. *Police Chief, 55* (No. 11): 20–22, 1988.

Schwartz, Jeffrey A., and Schwartz, Cynthia B.: The personal problems of the police officer: A plea for action. In Territo, Leonard, and Vetter, Harold J. (Eds.): *Stress and Police Personnel.* Boston, Allyn and Bacon, 99–113, 1981.

Seligman, Tom: How good are women cops? *Parade Magazine, Seattle Times:* 5–7, March 31, 1985.

Sherman, Lawrence W.: Causes of police behavior: The current state of quantitative research. In Blumberg, Abraham S., and Niederhoffer, Elaine (Eds.): *The Ambivalent Force: Perspectives on the Police,* 3rd ed. New York, Holt, Rinehart and Winston, 183–195, 1985.

Silbert, Mimi H.: Job stress and burnout of new police officers. *Police Chief, 49* (No. 6): 46–48, 1982.

Skolnick, Jerome H., and Bayley, David H.: *The New Blue Line: Police Innovation in Six American Cities.* New York, Free Press, 1986.

Snortum, John R., and Beyers, John C.: Patrol activities of male and female officers as a function of work experience. *Police Studies, 6* (No. 1): 36–42, 1983.

State, local governments refusing to alter existing affirmative action programs. *Crime Control Digest, 19* (No. 22): 3–4, June 3, 1985.

Steel, Brent S., and Lovrich, Nicholas P.: Equality and efficiency tradeoffs in affirmative action—real or imagined? The case of women in policing. *Social Science Journal, 24:* 53–70, 1987.

Steffensmeier, Darrell J.: Sex role orientation and attitudes toward female police. *Police Studies, 2* (No. 1): 39–42, 1979.

Steinbeck, Katherine: Women in law enforcement. *Campus Law Enforcement Journal, 15* (No. 1): 12–15, 1985.

Stickley, A. Vance: Women supervising men. *WomenPolice, 21:* 9, December 1987.

Stickley, A. Vance: Women in command. *WomenPolice, 22:* 8–9, June 1988.

Stickley, A. Vance: Women in command. *WomenPolice, 22:* 8–9, 15, September 1988.

Taubman, Bryna: *Lady Cop.* New York, Warner Books, 1987.

Townsey, Roi D.: Black women in American policing: An advancement display. *Journal of Criminal Justice, 10:* 455–468, 1982 (a).

Townsey, Roi D.: Female patrol officers: A review of the physical capability issue. In Price, Barbara R. and Sokoloff, Natalie J. (Eds.): *The Criminal Justice System and Women: Women Offenders, Victims, Workers.* New York, Clark Boardman, 413–425, 1982 (b).

Ubell, Earl: Is your job killing you? *Parade Magazine, Seattle Times:* 4–7, January 8, 1989.

Ullman, Robert N.: Policewomen are special. *Law and Order, 32* (No. 4): 70–71, 1984.

Vastola, Anthony: Selecting patrol car partners: Implications for productivity in policing. *Police Chief, 47* (No. 1): 40–41, 1980.

van Wormer, Katharine: Are males suited to police patrol work? *Police Studies, 3* (No. 4): 41–44, 1981.

Vega, Manuel, and Silverman, Ira J.: Female police officers as viewed by their male counterparts. *Police Studies, 5* (No. 1): 31–39, 1982.

Voswinkel, Mary M.: Women in policing: What's the issue? *Campus Law Enforcement Journal, 15* (No. 1): 16–17, 1985.

Walker, Samuel: Racial minority and female employment in policing: The implications of "glacial" change. *Crime and Delinquency, 31:* 555–572, 1985.

Washington, Brenda: Stress and the female officer. In Territo, Leonard, and Vetter, Harold J. (Eds.): *Stress and Police Personnel.* Boston, Allyn and Bacon, 142–147, 1981.

Weber, Dick: New honor for Rulette Armstead. *San Diego Union,* B-3, April 20, 1989.

Weisheit, Ralph A.: Women in the state police: Concerns of male and female officers. *Journal of Police Science and Administration, 15:* 137–144, 1987.

Weisheit, Ralph A., and Mahan, Sue: *Women, Crime, and Criminal Justice.* Cincinnati, Anderson, 1988.

Wexler, Judie G.: Role styles of women police officers. *Sex Roles, 12:* 749–755, 1985.

Wexler, Judie G., and Logan, Deana D.: Sources of stress among women police officers. *Journal of Police Science and Administration, 11:* 46–53, 1983.

Wexler, Judie G., and Quinn, Vicki: Considerations in the training and development of women sergeants. *Journal of Police Science and Administration, 13:* 98–105, 1985.

Winnard, Karin E.: Policewomen and the people they serve. *Police Chief, 53* (No. 8): 62–63, 1986.

Women make good police concludes ex-Chicago cop. *Police Chief, 48* (No. 3): 11, 1981.

Young, Caroline: Top cop, super mom. *Seattle Post-Intelligencer:* F4, October 9, 1988.

Zytowski, Donald G.: Kuder Occupational Interest Survey scores and self-descriptive information on 348 women police. Unpublished raw data. 1989.

Zytowski, Donald G., and Isgro, Kathleen G.: Results of the Kuder Interest Survey. *WomenPolice, 22:* 9, 1988.

AUTHOR INDEX

199

SUBJECT INDEX